ESSENTIAL

PIANO EXERCISES

Every Piano Player Should Know
(second edition)

Learn Intervals, Pentascales, Tetrachords, Scales (major and minor),
Chords (triads, sus, aug., dim., 6th, 7th), Chord Progressions, and FUN, COOL Piano
Exercises in all Key Signatures and in all inversions.

Music Mentor

JERALD SIMON

Learn how to play piano the FUN way!
The Apprentice Stage™- The Maestro Stage™ - The Virtuoso Stage™

Music Motivation®
musicmotivation.com
Music that excites, entertains, and educates! ™

Music Motivation® books are designed to provide students with music instruction that will enable them to improve and increase their successes in the field of music. It is also intended to enhance appreciation and understanding of various styles of music from classical to jazz, blues, rock, popular, new age, hymns, and more. The author and publisher disclaim any liability or accountability for the misuse of this material as it was intended by the author.

I hope you enjoy **"Essential Piano Exercises"**. With this book, [I] hope piano teachers and piano students learn what I feel are th[e] essentials that everyone who plays the piano should know and b[e] able to do well. I don't want teachers and students to simply read th[e] notes on the page. I would like everyone who plays these exercise[s] to know them inside and out. There are quite a few addition[al] books in this series - and more to come. If you like this boo[k] please look at my other books: **"Essential Jazz Piano Exercises Ever[y] Piano Player Should Know," "Essential New Age Piano Exercise[s] Every Piano Player Should Know," "100 Left Hand Patterns Ever[y] Piano Player Should Know,"** and **"100 Chord Progressions Ever[y] Piano Player Should Know."** I hope you enjoy these various book[s]. You can learn more at **http://essentialpianoexercises.com**.

Your Music Mentor Jerald Simo[n]

This book is dedicated to my many piano students, young and old, who have asked me over the years to put together a book with all of the piano exercises I feel are essential to help them play better in all keys and in all inversions. Also, for my wife, Suzanne (Zanny), my daughter, Summer, and my sons, Preston and Matthew.

CONNECT with Jerald

http://musicmotivation.com/jeraldsimon
https://facebook.com/jeraldsimon
http://youtube.com/jeraldsimon
http://linkedin.com/in/jeraldsimon
http://pinterest.com/jeraldsimon
https://twitter.com/jeraldsimon
http://cdbaby.com/artist/jeraldsimon
http://instagram.com/jeraldsimon
jeraldsimon@musicmotivation.com

CONTACT Music Motivation®

Music Motivation®
Cool music that excites, entertains, and educates!

Music Motivation®
P.O. Box 1000
Kaysville, UT 84037-1000
http://musicmotivation.com
https://facebook.com/musicmotivation
https://twitter.com/musicmotivation
info@musicmotivation.com

First Printing 2015 - Originally created from 2006-2020 - Printed in the United States of America - 10 9 8 7 6 5 4 3 2 - Simon, Jerald - Music Motivation® Essential Piano Exercises - $29.95 US/ $31.95 Canada - Soft cover spiral bound book - ISBN-13: 978-1-948274-12-8 ; MM00001069

Music Motivation® is a registered ® trademark

Welcome to "ESSENTIAL PIANO EXERCISES" by JERALD SIMON

To better help piano teachers, piano students, and parents of piano students effectively learn the music theory and what to do with that knowledge, thus bridging the gap between learning the scales and chords and using them to enhance the music, and make music of your own, I have created a course featuring step by step piano lesson videos to accompany this book: "Essential Piano Exercises." You can visit **ESSENTIALPIANOEXERCISES. COM** to learn more about this course and gain access to the hundreds of videos where I demonstrate how to play these exercises and then teach what you can do with them. Learning the theory is good, but knowing what to do with it is the practical application where I demonstrate how to use music theory to arrange, to improvise, to compose, and to create music of your own. More important than simply learning the theory is the practical application of *why* we are learning these scales and chords, and *what* we can do with them once we have learned them. It is the hands on approach to teaching music theory. In addition, I explain the theory in practical and simple terms so everyone can easily understand and know music theory for what it can do to help them in three primary ways: (1) sight-read the piano music better and faster as a result of knowing the scales and chords, (2) take their music playing and music creating to the next level so they can improvise, arrange, and compose music of their own, and (3) ultimately feel comfortable and excited to learn music theory - the "FUN way!"

"My purpose and mission in life is to motivate myself and others through my music and writing, to help others find their purpose and mission in life, and to teach values that encourage everyone everywhere to do and be their best." - Jerald Simon

A message from Jerald to piano students and parents:

If you come to piano lessons each week and walk away only having learned about music notation, rhythm, and dots on a page, then I have failed as a Music Mentor. Life lessons are just as important, if not more important than music lessons. I would rather have you learn more about goal setting and achieving, character, dedication, and personal improvement. To have you learn to love music, appreciate it, and play it, is a wonderful byproduct you will have for the rest of your life - a talent that will enrich your life and the lives of others. To become a better musician is wonderful and important, but to become a better person is more important.

As a Music Mentor I want to mentor students to be the very best they can be. If you choose not to practice, you essentially choose not to improve. This is true in any area of life. Everyone has the same amount of time allotted to them. What you choose to do with your time, and where you spend your time, has little to do with the activities being done and more to do with the value attached to each activity.

I believe it's important to be well-rounded and have many diverse interests. I want students to enjoy music, to learn to be creative and understand how to express themselves musically - either by creating music of their own, or interpreting the music of others - by arranging and improvising well known music. In addition, I encourage students to play sports, dance, sing, draw, read, and develop all of their talents. I want them to be more than musicians, I want them to learn to become well-rounded individuals.

Above all, I want everyone to continually improve and do their best. I encourage everyone to set goals, dream big, and be the best they can be in whatever they choose to do. Life is full of wonderful choices. Choose the best out of life and learn as much as you can from everyone everywhere. I prefer being called a Music Mentor because I want to mentor others and help them to live their dreams.

Your life is your musical symphony. Make it a masterpiece!

This book was created to encourage all pianists, piano teachers, and piano students to play all scales and chords in all key signatures.

All of the scales (pentascales and major and minor scales) are presented following the circle of 5ths - moving from the key of C to G, and then on to D, A, E, B, F sharp, and C sharp. The pattern for playing the scales is best taught by following the circle of fifths (unless you are learning jazz scales, and then you might want to consider following the circle/cycle of fourths and playing the key signatures according to the flats - C to F, and then on to B flat, E flat, A flat, D flat, G flat, and C flat.

Essentially all pianists should be able to play all of these exercises in this book, in all key signatures moving in all directions following the circle of 5ths, following the circle/cycle of 4ths, moving up chromatically in half steps, or zig-zagging in any conceivable direction or order (e.g. following chord progressions or moving through random key signatures at will).

All of the exercises with chords - all triads (three note chords) and all sixth and seventh chords are presented moving up chromatically (or in half steps). This is done because it is one of the best ways to teach the patterns of the chords as they move through key signatures. This helps students develop muscle memory to more quickly and easily change keys and play the chords in all inversions by developing a feel for the individual chords in all keys and in all inversions.

Everything taught in this book is presented based on the Music Motivation® Mentorship Map (on page five) and is something I personally created to let my piano students and their parents know what I would like to have them learn year by year, and what we would focus on, including: repertoire, music terminology, key signatures, music notation, rhythms, intervals, scales, modes, chords, arpeggios, inversions, technique, sight reading, ear training, music history, improvisation, and composition. It's quite thorough, and helps the students, parents, and piano teachers have a map, so to speak, to guide them on their musical journey.

On pages six and seven you will see the Music Motivation® Check List where I created a check off sheet to help students see what they have learned. On pages 8-12 we focus on learning the key signatures with a handout that piano students and piano teachers may make additional copies of (on page 10) to practice writing out all of the key signatures - major and minor - with all of the sharps and flats that go with each key signature.

Pages 13-58 feature all of the "Apprentice" level exercises that I have listed as appropriate for first and second year students. Starting on page 59 to the end of the book, I feature the exercises from the "Maestro" and "Virtuoso" levels.

Have a wonderful time playing these exercises and mastering all intervals, scales, and chords in all keys and in all inversions!

Music Mentor

JERALD SIMON

The *Music Motivation*® Mentorship Map (for piano students)
by Music Mentor™ Jerald Simon

Music Motivation® — musicmotivation.com

Left margin (vertical): This is only an outline or suggestion - add to it or subtract from it! If you are doing something different all together that works, keep doing it. This is meant to give you ideas and supplement what you're already doing.

Right margin (vertical): The books from the Music Motivation® Series by Jerald Simon are not method books, and are not intentionally created to be used as such (although some piano teachers use them as such). Jerald simply creates fun, cool piano music to motivate piano students to play the piano and teach them music theory - the FUN way!

	Apprentice (for 1st & 2nd year students)	Maestro (for 2nd - 4th year students)	Virtuoso (for 3rd year students and above)
Repertoire (In addition to the books listed to the right, students can sign up to receive the weekly "Cool Song" and "Cool Exercise" composed by Jerald Simon every week. Visit musicmotivation.com/annualsubscription to learn more and sign up!)	**Music Motivation® Book(s)** — What Every Pianist Should Know (Free PDF); Essential Piano Exercises (section 1); Cool Songs for Cool Kids (pre-primer level); Cool Songs for Cool Kids (primer level); Cool Songs for Cool Kids (book 1); The Pentascale Pop Star (books 1 and 2). Songs in Pentascale position: Classical, Jazz, Blues, Popular, Students Choice, Personal Composition (in pentascale position - 5 note piano solo) etc.	**Music Motivation® Book(s)** — Essential Piano Exercises (section 2); An Introduction to Scales and Modes; Cool Songs for Cool Kids (book 2); Cool Songs for Cool Kids (book 3); Variations on Mary Had a Little Lamb; Twinkle Those Stars, Jazzed about Christmas, Jazzed about 4th of July. Baroque, Romantic, Classical, Jazz, Blues, Popular, New Age, Student's Choice, Personal Composition.	**Music Motivation® Book(s)** — Essential Piano Exercises (section 3); Cool Songs that ROCK! (books 1 & 2); Triumphant, Sea Fever, Sweet Melancholy, The Dawn of a New Age, Sweet Modality, Jazzed about Jazz, Jazzed about Classical Music, Jingle Those Bells, Cinematic Solos, Hymn Arranging. Baroque, Romantic, Classical, Jazz, Blues, Popular, New Age, Contemporary, Broadway Show Tunes, Standards, Student's Choice, Personal Composition
Music Terminology	Piano (*p*), Forte (*f*) Mezzo Piano (*mp*) Mezzo Forte (*mf*) Pianissimo (*pp*) Fortissimo (*ff*) *Music Motivation® 1st Year Terminology*	Tempo Markings; Dynamic Markings; Parts of the Piano; Styles and Genres of Music; *Music Motivation® 2nd Year Terminology*	Pocket Music Dictionary (2 - 3 years); Harvard Dictionary of Music (4 + years); Parts/History of the Piano; Music Composers (Weekly Biographies); *Music Motivation® 3rd Year Terminology*
Key Signatures	C, G, D, A, F, B♭, E♭ & A♭ (Major); A, E, B, F♯, D, G, C & F (Minor). Begin learning all major key signatures	Circle of 5ths/Circle of 4ths. <u>All</u> Major and Minor key signatures (Identify each key and name the sharps and flats)	Spiral of Fifths, Chord Progressions within Key Signatures. Modulating from one Key Signature to another.
Music Notation	Names and Positions of notes on the staff (both hands - Treble and Bass Clefs)	Names and Positions of notes above and below the staff (both hands)	History of Music Notation (the development of notation), Monks & Music, Gregorian Chants, Music changes over the years and how music has changed. Learn **Finale** and **Logic Pro** (notate your music)
Rhythms	Whole notes/rests (say it and play it - count out loud); Half notes/rests (say it and play it - count out loud); Quarter notes/rests (say it and play it - count out loud); Eighth notes/rests (say it and play it - count out loud)	Sixteenth notes/rests (say it and play it - count out loud); Thirty-second notes/rests (say it and play it - count out loud); Sixty-fourth notes/rests (say it and play it - count out loud)	One-hundred-twenty-eighth notes/rests. For more on rhythm, I recommend: "Rhythmic Training" by Robert Starer and "Logical Approach to Rhythmic Notation" (books 1 & 2) by Phil Perkins
Intervals	1st, 2nd, 3rd, 4th, 5th, 6th, 7th, 8th, and 9th intervals (key of C, G, D, F, B♭, and E♭). Harmonic and Melodic intervals (key of C, G, D, A, E, and B)	All Perfect, Major, Minor, Augmented, and Diminished intervals (in every key). All Harmonic and Melodic intervals. Explain the intervals used to create major, minor, diminished, and augmented chords?	9th, 11th, and 13th intervals. Analyze music (Hymns and Classical) to identify intervals used in each measure. Identify/Name intervals used in chords.
Scales	<u>All</u> Major Pentascales (5 finger scale); <u>All</u> Minor Pentascales (5 finger scale); <u>All</u> Diminished Pentascales (5 finger scale); C Major Scale (1 octave) A min. Scale (1 oct.) (Do, Re, Mi, Fa, Sol, La, Ti, Do) (solfege). All Major and Natural Minor Scales - 1 octave	<u>All</u> Major Scales (Every Key 1 - 2 octaves); <u>All</u> Minor Scales (Every Key 1 - 2 octaves) (natural, harmonic, and melodic minor scales). (Do, Di, Re, Ri, Mi, Fa, Fi, Sol, Si, La, Li, Ti, Do) (solfege - chromatic)	<u>All</u> Major Scales (Every Key 3 - 5 Octaves); <u>All</u> Minor Scales (Every Key 3 - 5 Octaves); <u>All</u> Blues Scales (major and minor); Cultural Scales (25 + scales)
Modes	Ionian/Aeolian (C/A, G/E, D/B, A/F♯)	<u>All</u> Modes (I, D, P, L, M, A, L) <u>All</u> keys	Modulating with the Modes (Dorian to Dorian)
Chords	<u>All</u> Major Chords, <u>All</u> Minor Chords, <u>All</u> Diminished Chords, C Sus 2, C Sus 4, C+ (Aug.), C 6th, C minor 6th, C 7th, C Maj. 7th, C minor Major 7th, A min., A Sus 2, A Sus 4,	All Major, Minor, Diminished, Augmented, Sus 2, Sus 4, Sixth, Minor Sixth, Dominant 7th and Major 7th Chords	Review <u>All</u> Chords from 1st and 2nd year experiences. <u>All</u> 7th, 9th, 11th, and 13th chords inversions and voicings.
Arpeggios	Same chords as above (1 - 2 octaves)	Same chords as above (3 - 4 octaves)	Same chords as above (4 + octaves)
Inversions	Same chords as above (1 - 2 octaves)	Same chords as above (3 - 4 octaves)	Same chords as above (4 + octaves)
Technique (other)	Schmitt Preparatory Exercises, (Hanon)	Wieck, Hanon, Bach (well tempered clavier)	Bertini-Germer, Czerny, I. Philipp
Sight Reading	Key of C Major and G Major	Key of C, G, D, A, E, F, B♭, E♭, A♭, D♭	<u>All</u> Key Signatures, Hymns, Classical
Ear Training	Major versus Minor sounds (chords/intervals)	C, D, E, F, G, A, B, and intervals	Key Signatures and Chords, Play w/ IPod
Music History	The origins of the Piano Forte	Baroque, Classical, Jazz, Blues	Students choice - <u>All</u> genres, Composers
Improvisation	Mary Had a Little Lamb, Twinkle, Twinkle...	Blues Pentascale, Barrelhouse Blues	Classical, New Age, Jazz, Blues, etc. Play w/ IPod
Composition	5 note melody (both hands - key of C and G)	One - Two Page Song (include key change)	Lyrical, Classical, New Age, Jazz, etc.

Copyright © 2020 by Music Motivation® - http://musicmotivation.com

5

Music Motivation® Check List

- Check off when completed -
(follow the circle of 5ths/4ths - or move up in half steps - you should be able to do all three)

The boxes below and on the other side of this page should be checked off as completed when the piano student can successfully complete each exercise in a given key signature, up to speed, and with no mistakes.

Following the circle of fifths — All Key Signatures & Pentascales

All Major Key Signatures: (tell your teacher the # of sharps/flats in each key and what they are)

C	G	D	A	E	B / C♭	F♯ / G♭	C♯ / D♭	A♭	E♭	B♭	F
☐	☐	☐	☐	☐	☐	☐	☐	☐	☐	☐	☐

All Minor Key Signatures: (tell your teacher the # of sharps/flats in each key and what they are)

a	e	b	f♯	c♯	g♯ / a♭	d♯ / e♭	a♯ / b♭	f	c	g	d
☐	☐	☐	☐	☐	☐	☐	☐	☐	☐	☐	☐

All Major Pentascales: Quarter Notes and Eighth Notes

C	G	D	A	E	B / C♭	F♯ / G♭	C♯ / D♭	A♭	E♭	B♭	F
☐	☐	☐	☐	☐	☐	☐	☐	☐	☐	☐	☐

All Minor Pentascales: Quarter Notes and Eighth Notes

a	e	b	f♯	c♯	g♯ / a♭	d♯ / e♭	a♯ / b♭	f	c	g	d
☐	☐	☐	☐	☐	☐	☐	☐	☐	☐	☐	☐

All Diminished Pentascales: Quarter Notes and Eighth Notes

a	e	b	f♯	c♯	g♯ / a♭	d♯ / e♭	a♯ / b♭	f	c	g	d
☐	☐	☐	☐	☐	☐	☐	☐	☐	☐	☐	☐

Following the circle of fifths — Intervals & Major/Minor Scales

Intervals (built from all major scales) (1st, 2nd, 3rd, 4th, 5th, 6th, 7th, 8th):

C	G	D	A	E	B / C♭	F♯ / G♭	C♯ / D♭	A♭	E♭	B♭	F
☐	☐	☐	☐	☐	☐	☐	☐	☐	☐	☐	☐

All Major Scales (1 octave): (parallel and contrary motion)

C	G	D	A	E	B / C♭	F♯ / G♭	C♯ / D♭	A♭	E♭	B♭	F
☐	☐	☐	☐	☐	☐	☐	☐	☐	☐	☐	☐

All Minor Scales (1 octave): (natural, harmonic, and melodic)

a	e	b	f♯	c♯	g♯ / a♭	d♯ / e♭	a♯ / b♭	f	c	g	d
☐	☐	☐	☐	☐	☐	☐	☐	☐	☐	☐	☐

All Major Scales (2-4 octaves): NO MUSIC PROVIDED - play without music

C	G	D	A	E	B / C♭	F♯ / G♭	C♯ / D♭	A♭	E♭	B♭	F
☐	☐	☐	☐	☐	☐	☐	☐	☐	☐	☐	☐

All Minor Scales (2-4 octaves): NO MUSIC PROVIDED - play without music

a	e	b	f♯	c♯	g♯ / a♭	d♯ / e♭	a♯ / b♭	f	c	g	d
☐	☐	☐	☐	☐	☐	☐	☐	☐	☐	☐	☐

Moving up chromatically (in half steps) — All Triads (three note chords)

All Major Triads: (root, 1st, and 2nd inversions)

C	C♯ / D♭	D	E♭	E	F	F♯ / G♭	G	A♭	A	B♭	B / C♭
☐	☐	☐	☐	☐	☐	☐	☐	☐	☐	☐	☐

All Minor Triads: (root, 1st, and 2nd inversions)

C	C♯ / D♭	D	E♭	E	F	F♯ / G♭	G	A♭	A	B♭	B / C♭
☐	☐	☐	☐	☐	☐	☐	☐	☐	☐	☐	☐

All Diminished Triads: (root, 1st, and 2nd inversions)

C	C♯ / D♭	D	E♭	E	F	F♯ / G♭	G	A♭	A	B♭	B / C♭
☐	☐	☐	☐	☐	☐	☐	☐	☐	☐	☐	☐

All Augmented Triads: (root, 1st, and 2nd inversions)

C	C♯ / D♭	D	E♭	E	F	F♯ / G♭	G	A♭	A	B♭	B / C♭
☐	☐	☐	☐	☐	☐	☐	☐	☐	☐	☐	☐

All Sus4 Triads: (root, 1st, and 2nd inversions)

C	C♯ / D♭	D	E♭	E	F	F♯ / G♭	G	A♭	A	B♭	B / C♭
☐	☐	☐	☐	☐	☐	☐	☐	☐	☐	☐	☐

All Sus2 Triads: (root, 1st, and 2nd inversions)

C	C♯ / D♭	D	E♭	E	F	F♯ / G♭	G	A♭	A	B♭	B / C♭
☐	☐	☐	☐	☐	☐	☐	☐	☐	☐	☐	☐

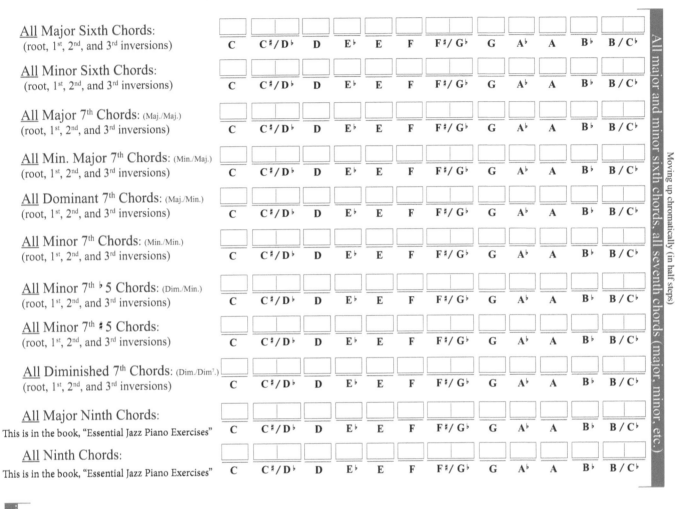

All major and minor sixth chords, all seventh chords (major, minor, etc.)
Moving up chromatically (in half steps)

Chord Type	C	C#/Db	D	Eb	E	F	F#/Gb	G	Ab	A	Bb	B/Cb
All Major Sixth Chords: (root, 1st, 2nd, and 3rd inversions)												
All Minor Sixth Chords: (root, 1st, 2nd, and 3rd inversions)												
All Major 7th Chords: (Maj./Maj.) (root, 1st, 2nd, and 3rd inversions)												
All Min. Major 7th Chords: (Min./Maj.) (root, 1st, 2nd, and 3rd inversions)												
All Dominant 7th Chords: (Maj./Min.) (root, 1st, 2nd, and 3rd inversions)												
All Minor 7th Chords: (Min./Min.) (root, 1st, 2nd, and 3rd inversions)												
All Minor 7th ♭5 Chords: (Dim./Min.) (root, 1st, 2nd, and 3rd inversions)												
All Minor 7th ♯5 Chords: (root, 1st, 2nd, and 3rd inversions)												
All Diminished 7th Chords: (Dim./Dim7.) (root, 1st, 2nd, and 3rd inversions)												
All Major Ninth Chords: This is in the book, "Essential Jazz Piano Exercises"												
All Ninth Chords: This is in the book, "Essential Jazz Piano Exercises"												

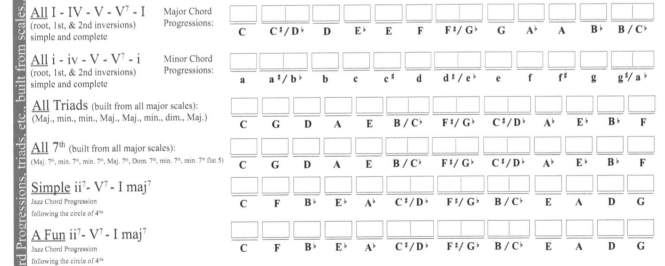

Chord Progressions, triads, etc. built from scales...
These last two are in the book, "Essential Jazz Piano Exercises" by Jerald Simon

All I - IV - V - V⁷ - I (root, 1st, & 2nd inversions) simple and complete — Major Chord Progressions:

C	C#/Db	D	Eb	E	F	F#/Gb	G	Ab	A	Bb	B/Cb

All i - iv - V - V⁷ - i (root, 1st, & 2nd inversions) simple and complete — Minor Chord Progressions:

a	a#/bb	b	c	c#	d	d#/eb	e	f	f#	g	g#/ab

All Triads (built from all major scales): (Maj., min., min., Maj., Maj., min., dim., Maj.)

C	G	D	A	E	B/Cb	F#/Gb	C#/Db	Ab	Eb	Bb	F

All 7th (built from all major scales): (Maj. 7th, min. 7th, min. 7th, Maj. 7th, Dom. 7th, min. 7th, min. 7th flat 5)

C	G	D	A	E	B/Cb	F#/Gb	C#/Db	Ab	Eb	Bb	F

Simple ii⁷- V⁷ - I maj⁷ Jazz Chord Progression following the circle of 4ths

C	F	Bb	Eb	Ab	C#/Db	F#/Gb	B/Cb	E	A	D	G

A Fun ii⁷- V⁷ - I maj⁷ Jazz Chord Progression following the circle of 4ths

C	F	Bb	Eb	Ab	C#/Db	F#/Gb	B/Cb	E	A	D	G

In the book, *"Essential Jazz Piano Exercises,"* we cover 9th chords, 11th chords, 13th chords, voicings of chords, blues scales (major and minor), left hand patterns (walking bass patterns, boogie-woogie patterns, etc.), modal jazz improvisation, ii-V-I chord progressions, ii-V chord progressions (dorian - dorian), and much more. The book, "Essential New Age Piano Exercises," introduces new age patterns.

Key Signatures (Major and Minor) and Major Penta Scales, and Scales:

(Circle of Fifths)

Let's talk about key signatures. When we talk about key signatures, the easiest way to explain them is by thinking about languages.

Look at the chart of the circle of fifths on the next two pages in the handout. In the key of C major we have no sharps or flats. If we move to the right of the circle of fifths we will be in the key signature of G major. Think of this like learning to speak German. We have one sharp - F sharp (F♯) in the key signature. When we are playing a piece in the key of G major we will always have an F sharp (everytime you see F play F sharp (F♯) instead of F natural).

Any note in the musical alphabet (A, B, C, D, E, F, and G) can have a flat sign (♭) or a sharp sign (♯) placed in front of it. When this happens, the note either moves down half a step to the left for flats, or up half a step to the right for sharps. Let's look at the F note. The regular F note is the fourth above C. The F note is a white note, but when it has a sharp placed in front of it the note is taken up half a step to the right. The black note directly to the right of F is F sharp (F♯).

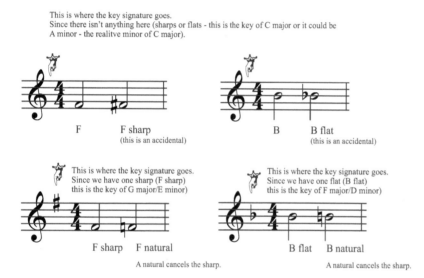

The first example to the left is in the key of C major. When the sharp symbol (♯) is added in the measure you will play the sharp for that measure only. This is called an accidental note because it is not part of the key signature. After you finish playing the measure with the sharp, you will play the F natural again unless you see another accidental note. Below the first example is an example of the key of G major (which has an F sharp in the key signature) followed by an F natural. The same examples are shown with B flat and B natural.

I like to have the students memorize the order of the sharps introduced by saying this:

Five **C**ool **G**orrilas **D**ance **A**nd **E**at **B**annanas. Once they have memorized this saying I tell them the order of the sharps is F♯, C♯, G♯, D♯, A♯, E♯ and B♯. For flats I have them say: **B**etter **E**xercise **A**nd **D**rink **G**ood **C**old **F**luids. Once they have memorized this saying I tell them the order of the flats as B♭, E♭, A♭, D♭, G♭, C♭, and F♭.

♯ 🖎 **Memorize This!** for key signatures with sharps: **F**ive **C**ool **G**orrilas **D**ance **A**nd **E**at **B**annanas.

♭ 🖎 **Memorize This!** for key signatures with flats: **B**etter **E**xercise **A**nd **D**rink **G**ood **C**old **F**luids
(for flats you may also say BEAD GCF if that helps you)

I like to have students first play all major pentascales in all keys following the circle of fifths. After they can play all of the major pentascales in all keys, I then have them learn the minor and diminished pentascales in all keys. They can learn the patterns and the feel of playing the pentascales in all keys quickly. After doing so they are then ready to play the major and minor scales 1 octave, then 2, and 3 octaves contrary (opposite direction starting on the same note - right hand goes up, left hand goes down, and parallel motion (both hand moving the same direction up and down the piano). I like to start with contrary motion because the fingering is the same for both hands and students learn the patterns quickly.

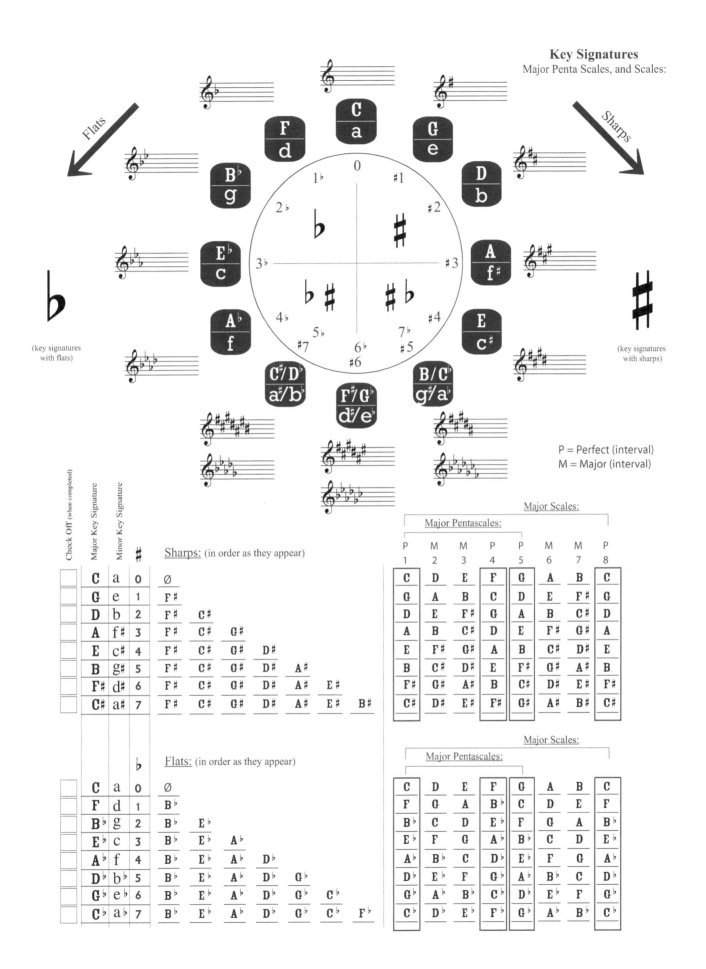

Key Signatures
Major Penta Scales, and Scales:

Flats

Sharps

(key signatures with flats)

(key signatures with sharps)

P = Perfect (interval)
M = Major (interval)

Major Scales:

Major Pentascales:

Check Off (when completed)	Major Key Signature	Minor Key Signature	#	Sharps: (in order as they appear)						
	C	a	0	Ø						
	G	e	1	F#						
	D	b	2	F#	C#					
	A	f#	3	F#	C#	G#				
	E	c#	4	F#	C#	G#	D#			
	B	g#	5	F#	C#	G#	D#	A#		
	F#	d#	6	F#	C#	G#	D#	A#	E#	
	C#	a#	7	F#	C#	G#	D#	A#	E#	B#

P 1	M 2	M 3	P 4	P 5	M 6	M 7	P 8
C	D	E	F	G	A	B	C
G	A	B	C	D	E	F#	G
D	E	F#	G	A	B	C#	D
A	B	C#	D	E	F#	G#	A
E	F#	G#	A	B	C#	D#	E
B	C#	D#	E	F#	G#	A#	B
F#	G#	A#	B	C#	D#	E#	F#
C#	D#	E#	F#	G#	A#	B#	C#

Major Scales:

Major Pentascales:

	Major Key Signature	Minor Key Signature	b	Flats: (in order as they appear)						
	C	a	0	Ø						
	F	d	1	Bb						
	Bb	g	2	Bb	Eb					
	Eb	c	3	Bb	Eb	Ab				
	Ab	f	4	Bb	Eb	Ab	Db			
	Db	bb	5	Bb	Eb	Ab	Db	Gb		
	Gb	eb	6	Bb	Eb	Ab	Db	Gb	Cb	
	Cb	ab	7	Bb	Eb	Ab	Db	Gb	Cb	Fb

C	D	E	F	G	A	B	C
F	G	A	Bb	C	D	E	F
Bb	C	D	Eb	F	G	A	Bb
Eb	F	G	Ab	Bb	C	D	Eb
Ab	Bb	C	Db	Eb	F	G	Ab
Db	Eb	F	Gb	Ab	Bb	C	Db
Gb	Ab	Bb	Cb	Db	Eb	F	Gb
Cb	Db	Eb	Fb	Gb	Ab	Bb	Cb

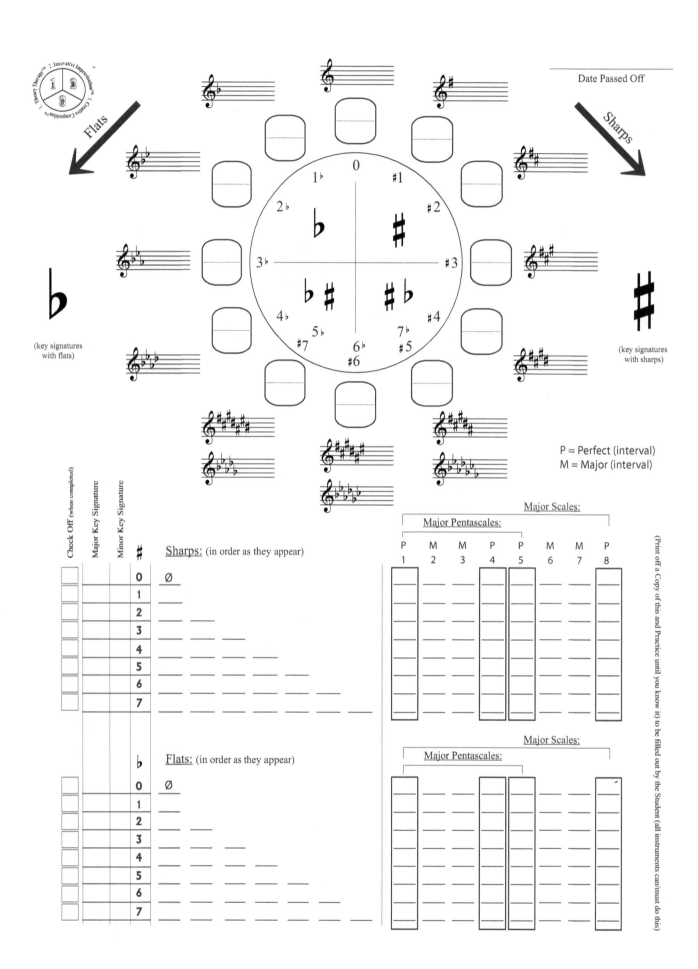

All Major Key Signatures

(following the circle of 5ths)

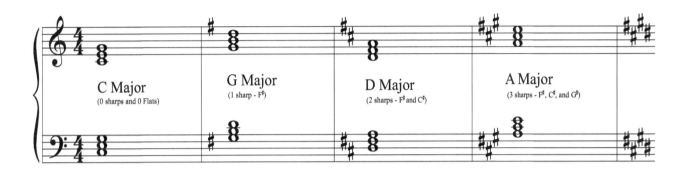

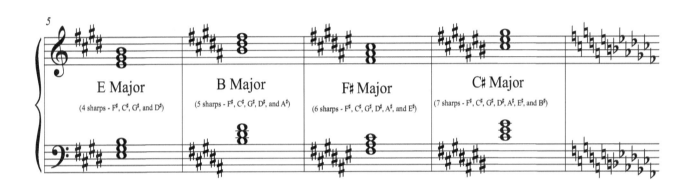

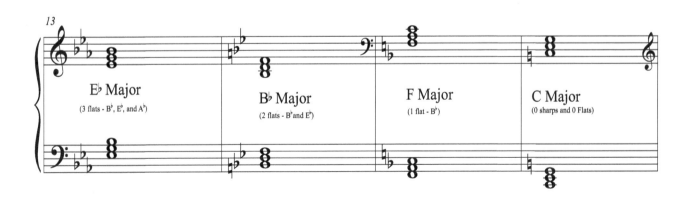

All Minor Key Signatures

(following the circle of 5ths)

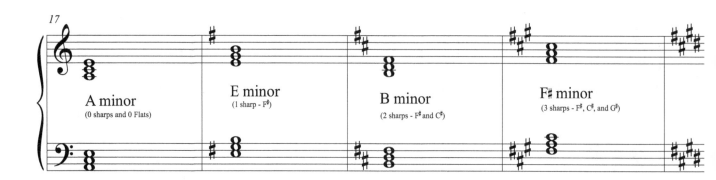

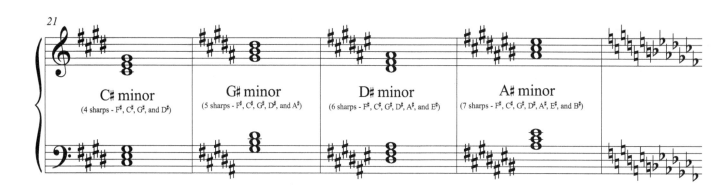

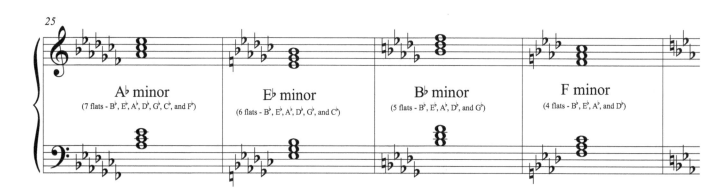

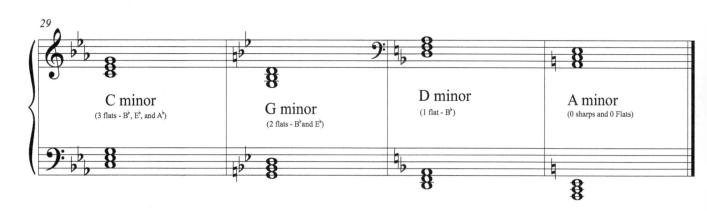

The "Apprentice Stage" begins on page 13 and continues until page 46.

These exercises are all in pentascale position, meaning they are all in a five finger position. The students should feel comfortable playing the five finger scales and intervals in all keys. It is a great way to develop the finger strength they need.

Music Terminology

Key Signatures

Music Notation

Rhythms

Intervals

Scales

Modes

Chords

Arpeggios

Inversions
Technique

Sight Reading
Ear Training
Music History
Improvisation
Composition

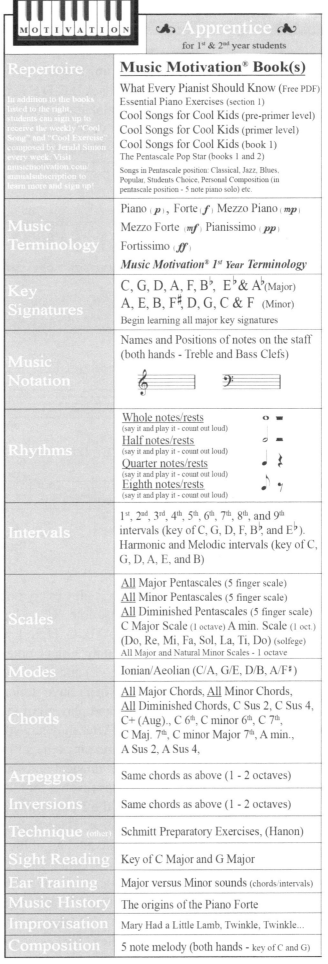

MOTIVATION

♫ Apprentice ♫
for 1st & 2nd year students

Repertoire	Music Motivation® Book(s)
In addition to the books listed to the right, students can sign up to receive the weekly "Cool Song" and "Cool Exercise" composed by Jerald Simon every week. Visit musicmotivation.com/annualsubscription to learn more and sign up!	What Every Pianist Should Know (Free PDF) Essential Piano Exercises (section 1) Cool Songs for Cool Kids (pre-primer level) Cool Songs for Cool Kids (primer level) Cool Songs for Cool Kids (book 1) The Pentascale Pop Star (books 1 and 2) Songs in Pentascale position: Classical, Jazz, Blues, Popular, Students Choice, Personal Composition (in pentascale position - 5 note piano solo) etc.
Music Terminology	Piano (p), Forte (f) Mezzo Piano (mp) Mezzo Forte (mf) Pianissimo (pp) Fortissimo (ff) *Music Motivation® 1st Year Terminology*
Key Signatures	C, G, D, A, F, B♭, E♭ & A♭ (Major) A, E, B, F♯, D, G, C & F (Minor) Begin learning all major key signatures
Music Notation	Names and Positions of notes on the staff (both hands - Treble and Bass Clefs)
Rhythms	Whole notes/rests (say it and play it - count out loud) Half notes/rests (say it and play it - count out loud) Quarter notes/rests (say it and play it - count out loud) Eighth notes/rests (say it and play it - count out loud)
Intervals	1st, 2nd, 3rd, 4th, 5th, 6th, 7th, 8th, and 9th intervals (key of C, G, D, F, B♭, and E♭). Harmonic and Melodic intervals (key of C, G, D, A, E, and B)
Scales	All Major Pentascales (5 finger scale) All Minor Pentascales (5 finger scale) All Diminished Pentascales (5 finger scale) C Major Scale (1 octave) A min. Scale (1 oct.) (Do, Re, Mi, Fa, Sol, La, Ti, Do) (solfege) All Major and Natural Minor Scales - 1 octave
Modes	Ionian/Aeolian (C/A, G/E, D/B, A/F♯)
Chords	All Major Chords, All Minor Chords, All Diminished Chords, C Sus 2, C Sus 4, C+ (Aug)., C 6th, C minor 6th, C 7th, C Maj. 7th, C minor Major 7th, A min., A Sus 2, A Sus 4,
Arpeggios	Same chords as above (1 - 2 octaves)
Inversions	Same chords as above (1 - 2 octaves)
Technique (other)	Schmitt Preparatory Exercises, (Hanon)
Sight Reading	Key of C Major and G Major
Ear Training	Major versus Minor sounds (chords/intervals)
Music History	The origins of the Piano Forte
Improvisation	Mary Had a Little Lamb, Twinkle, Twinkle...
Composition	5 note melody (both hands - key of C and G)

Essential Piano Exercises - Section ONE

❧ The Musical Alphabet ❧
A B C D E F and G

Learning music is similar to learning a foreign language. If you know your A B Cs, you already know the musical alphabet. The musical alphabet is A B C D E F and G. On the piano, the white note farthest to the left is A. That is the beginning of the musical alphabet. The white notes then continue as the alphabet does: A, B, C, D, E, F, and G. After G, it starts over again with A and continues up the piano (to the right).

The piano has a total of 88 keys. There are **52** white keys and **36** black keys. The note farthest to the left is A and the note farthest to the right is C. Here is what the **88** keys look like on a piano:

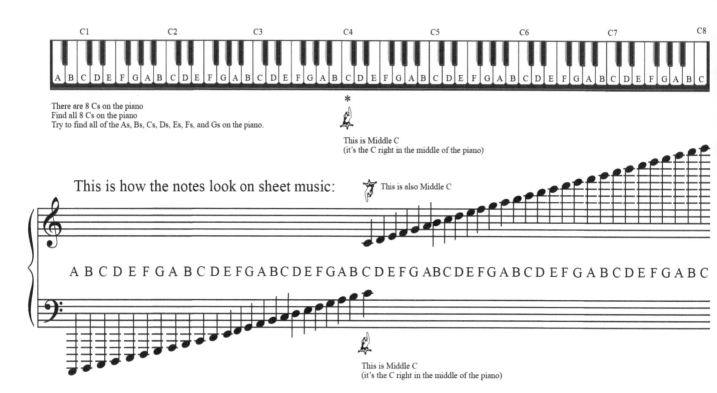

There are 8 Cs on the piano
Find all 8 Cs on the piano
Try to find all of the As, Bs, Cs, Ds, Es, Fs, and Gs on the piano.

This is Middle C
(it's the C right in the middle of the piano)

This is how the notes look on sheet music:

This is also Middle C

A B C D E F G A B C D E F G A B C D E F G A B C D E F G A B C D E F G A B C D E F G A B C D E F G A B C

This is Middle C
(it's the C right in the middle of the piano)

The first thing I have students do is play every note on the piano with one finger, starting with the lowest note "A" and continuing up to the highest note "C". I have students "Say it and Play it" - meaning they say the note name while they play the note (i.e. A, B, C, D, E, F, G, etc.). After they have done this, I have them find the pattern of 2 black notes together followed by 3 black notes together. I have students take two fingers with the left hand (the middle finger and the index finger) and play all of the 2 black note groups (both fingers play together at the same time) up and down the piano. Then I have students take three fingers with the right hand (the ring finger, the middle finger, and the index finger) and play all of the 3 black note groups (all three fingers play together at the same time) up and down the piano. After they have done this, students play with both hands (left hand plays the 2 black note groups then the right hand plays the 3 black note groups) up and down the piano.

I then teach easy ways to find the musical notes according to these black note group patterns. All Cs are found to the left of the 2 black note groups (except for the last C - farthest to the right). Have the students find all of the Cs. All Fs are found to the left of the 3 black note groups. Have the students find all of the Fs. All E's are found to the right of the 2 black note groups. Have the students find all of the Es. All Bs are found to the right of the 3 black note groups. Have the students find all of the Bs. Once students have found these notes, I have them find all of the Cs on the piano and play (with either hand) C D E F G. This is the C major pentascale (5 note scale). Have students find all of the Cs on the piano and have them play C D E F G, first with the left hand and then with the right hand or vice versa. Students should be able to identify all of the notes on the piano and find all of the As, Bs, Cs, Ds, Es, Fs, and Gs on the piano. Make sure they can play the C pentascale (C D E F G) beginning on each of the Cs of the piano (except for the C farthest to the right, of course).

Introduction

Watch your counting (M.M. ♩ = c. 120)

Have fun (Say it and Play it - count the rhythm out loud) play the right hand first, then the left hand, and then both hands together

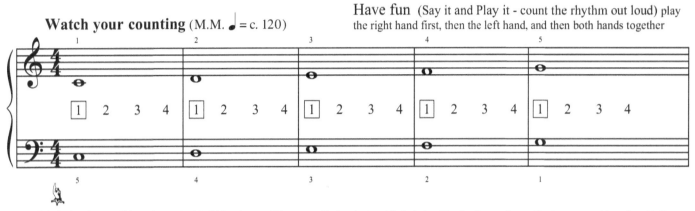

This is the time signature. This practice exercise is in 4/4 time signature. When you see this time signature at the beginning of the piece it means there are 4 beats per measure (clap and count to 4). The 4 on top means that there are 4 beats in each measure and the 4 on the bottom means that the quarter notes receive one beat. An easier way to explain this is by saying there are 4 quarter notes in every measure or something that equals 4 quarter notes.

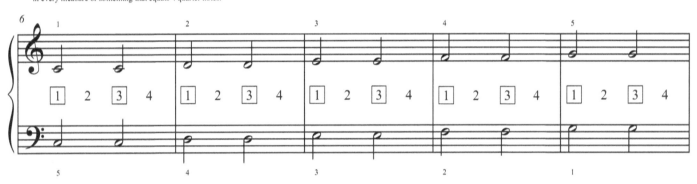

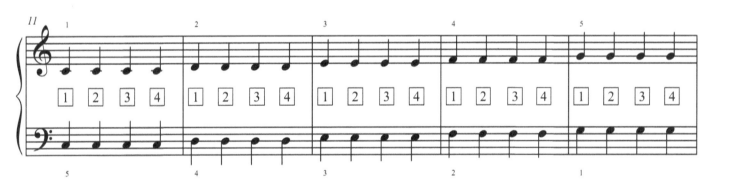

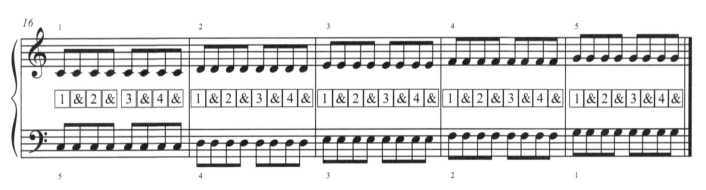

This exercise and some of the next few easy exercises are for beginning piano students and all of the exercises are taken from the Cool Songs for Cool Kids Primer level book by Jerald Simon ($14.95 - spiral bound book or $6.95 - PDF download of the book).

❧ Cool Piano Exercise #1 ❧

skill - C Major Pentascale (C D E F G), whole note, half note, quarter note, eighth note rhythms

Watch your counting (M.M. ♩ = c. 120)

Have Fun (Say it and Play it™ - count the rhythm out loud)

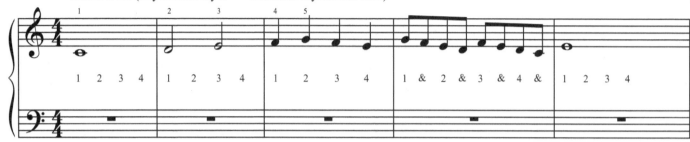

🐦 *Note to teacher, parent, or student:* When you **"Say it and Play it™"** you should do it two different ways: **(1)** Count out loud the rhythm as you play the piece (1 2 3 4, 1 & 2 & 3 & 4 &, etc.). This will help you learn the rhythm faster, how to count rhythm correctly, and how to quickly identify the note rhythms (i.e. whole note/half note/quarter note/eighth note, etc.). **(2)** Say the alphabet names of the notes you play (i.e. C D E F G F E G F E D F E D C E etc.).

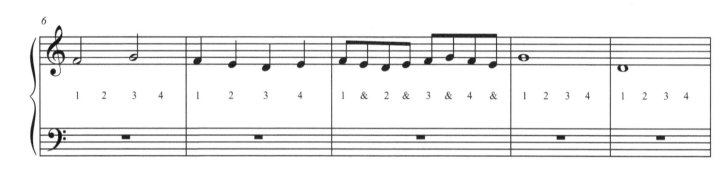

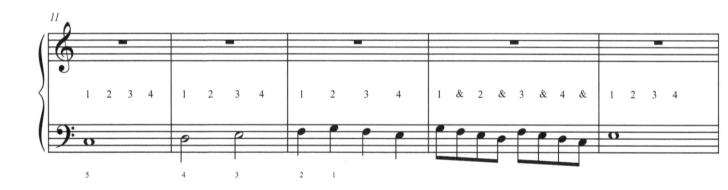

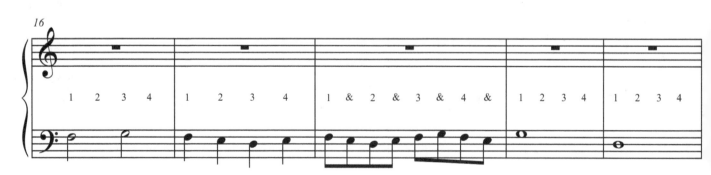

Cool Piano Exercise #1 (continued)

Play through this exercise several times before or after playing the previous exercise

ᔰ Cool Piano Exercise #2 ᔰ

Skill - blocked and broken intervals: 1st (i.e. C), 2nd (i.e. C and D), 3rd (i.e. C and E), 4th (i.e. C and F), 5th (i.e. C and G)

C - D is a second   C - E is a third   C - F is a fourth   C - G is a fifth

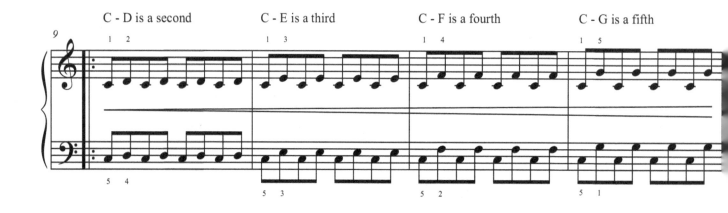

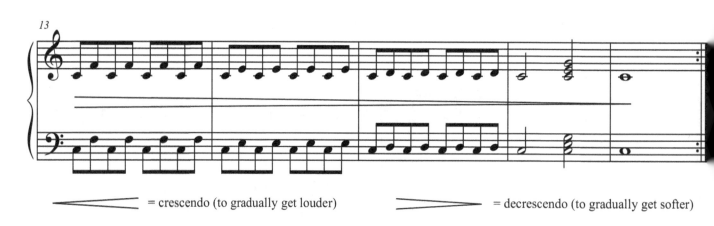

= crescendo (to gradually get louder)   = decrescendo (to gradually get softer)

Try playing this exercise. We're clumping notes together (in clusters). Your fingers are probably not used to moving like this. It may feel weird at first, but it will help.

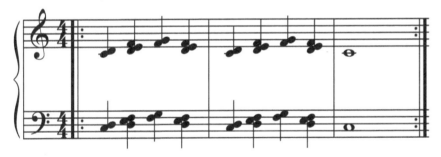

Try playing this exercise. This exercise helps your fingers learn to play well with each other. You don't want your fingers to fight each other. You want them to learn how to work well with each other.

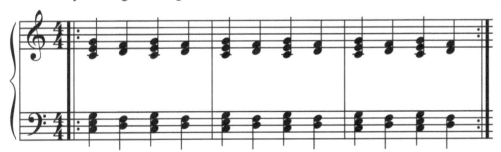

After playing the above exercise as written, move to the right and play it on starting on D, E, F, G, A, and B as well.

Cool Piano Exercise #3

Skill - blocked intervals: 1st (i.e. C), 2nd (i.e. C & D), 3rd (i.e. C & E), 4th (i.e. C & F), 5th (i.e. C & G)
C sus 2 (C suspend the 2nd chord), C (C Major chord), and C sus 4 (C suspend the 4th chord)

For fun, try playing this exercise and all of the "cool exercises" on pages 15-22 starting on C, D, E, F, G, A, and B as well - only playing the white keys though. It's a great way to practice moving up according to the C major scale, again, only playing the white keys.

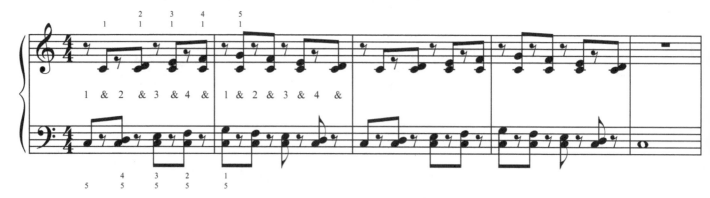

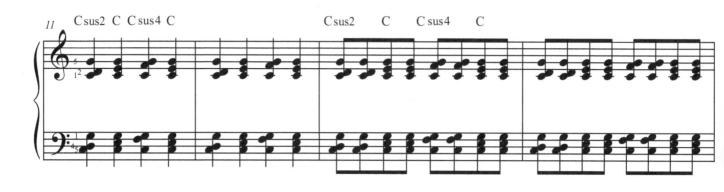

❧ Cool Piano Exercise #4 ❧

Skill - blocked intervals 5ᵗʰ (i.e. C and G), 6ᵗʰ (i.e. C and A), 7ᵗʰ (i.e. C and B) and 8ᵗʰ (i.e. C and C)
6/8 time signature

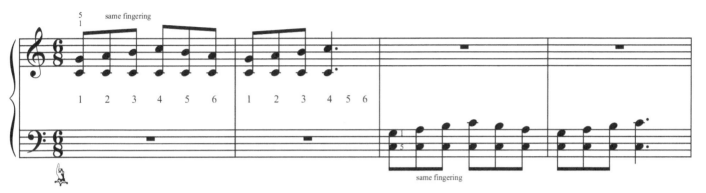

This is the 6/8 time signature. When you see this time signature at the beginning of the piece it means there are 6 beats per measure (clap and count to 6: 1 2 3 4 5 6). The 6 on top means that there are 6 beats in each measure and the 8 on the bottom means that the eighth notes receive one beat. An easier way to explain this is by saying there are 6 eighth notes in every measure or something that equals 6 eighth notes.

Practice playing blocked intervals 5ᵗʰ (i.e. C and G), 6ᵗʰ (i.e. C and A), 7ᵗʰ (i.e. C and B) and 8ᵗʰ (i.e. C and C).

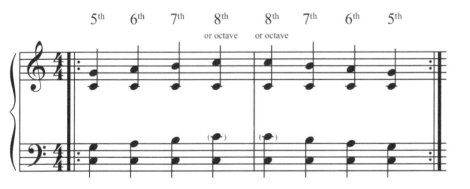

❧ Cool Piano Exercise #5 ❧

Skill - Triads (three note chords)

Play the triads created from the C major scale below (each of the triads begin on one of the notes from the C major scale - moving up one octave - C, D, E, F, G, A, B, and ending with C).

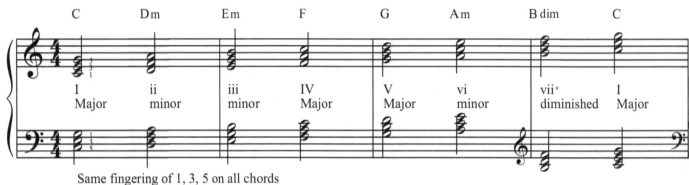

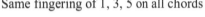

Same fingering of 1, 3, 5 on all chords

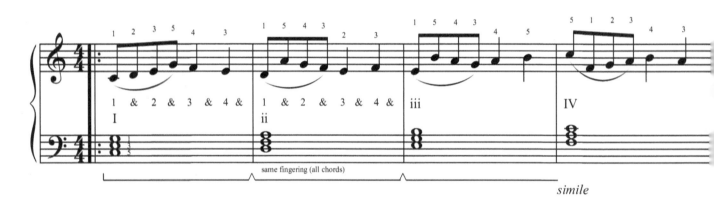

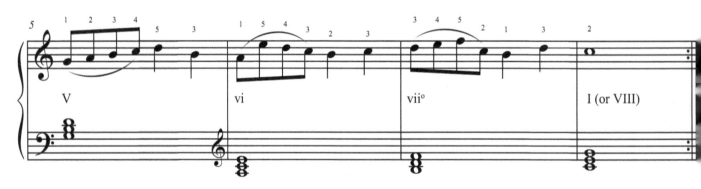

Right Hand ascends with intervals
Left Hand descends with intervals

This exercise features the prime (or unison) 1st interval, the major 2nd interval, the major 3rd interval, the perfect 4th interval, and the perfect 5th interval played as blocked (or harmonic) intervals.

After perfecting this exercise as it is written, for fun, try playing this exercise on all white keys starting on C, D, E, F, G, A, and B (simply move to the right one position on all of the white keys - and only use the white keys at first). After you have tried playing this on all white keys, try moving up half a step from C and play this exercise in all key signatures (moving up half a step each time - i.e. C sharp/D flat major, D major, E flat major, E major, etc.) according to the major scales of each key signature.

Skill - This exercise features the pentascale (five note scale) played with both hands followed by the triads (three note chords) - all moving up diatonically according to the C Major Scale. For fun you can try this in all keys following the major scales. I recommend following the Circle of 5ths (refer to page 9 from this book) and play this exercise in every key signature - adding one new sharp each time until you play this in every key. After you have played this in every key, try composing a simple piece of your own using the pentascale and the accompanying triads. It's fun! See what you can create!

Students can write in their own dynamics!

Same fingering for both hands throughout the exercise.

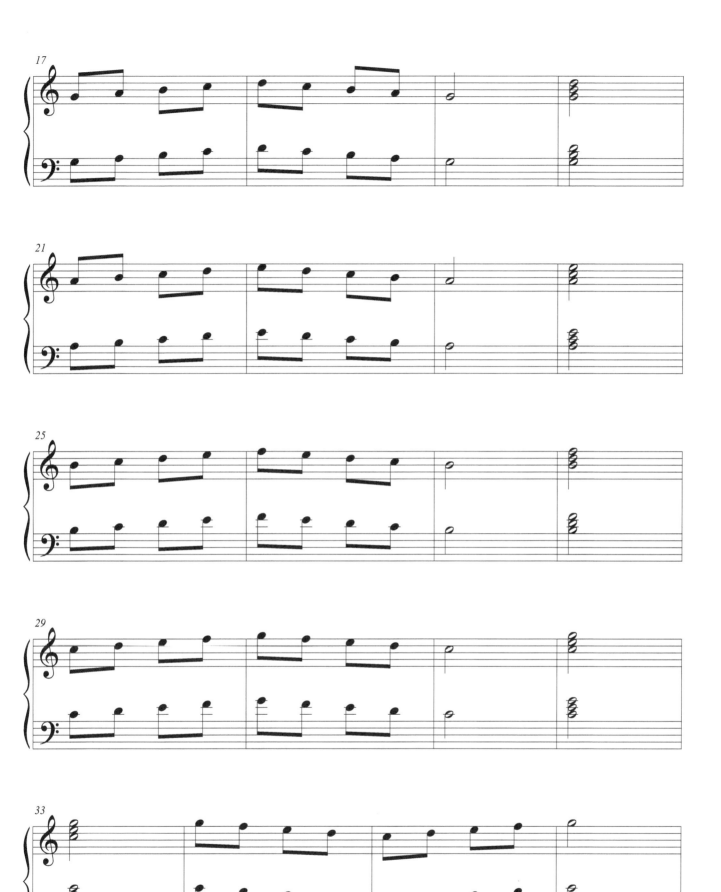

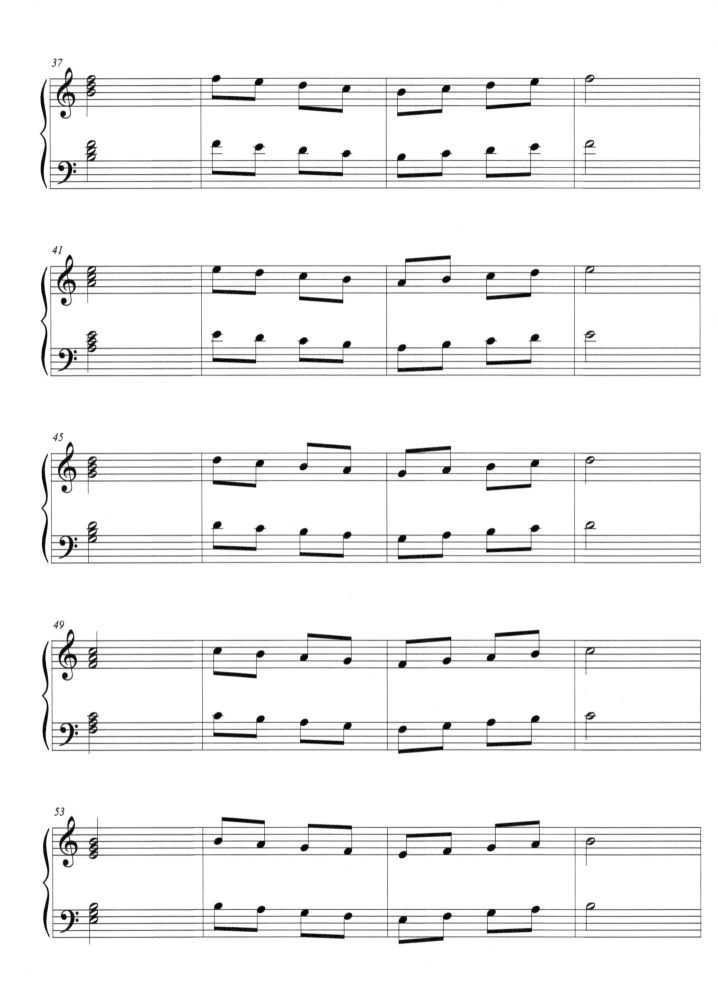

The word "interval" refers to the distance from one note to another. Intervals can be major, minor, perfect, augmented, or diminished in nature and quality. Intervals can also be played as melodic (or broken) intervals - meaning one note is played after another. Intervals can also be played as harmonic (or blocked) intervals - meaning both notes are played simultaneously at the same time. In this example, we are playing harmonic intervals (i.e. prime or unison 1st, {i.e. C} major 2nd {i.e. C and D}, major 3rd {i.e. C and E}, perfect 4th {i.e. C and F}, and perfect 5th {i.e. C and G} intervals.

Students can write in their own dynamics!

Same fingering for both hands throughout the exercise.

In this exercise we are playing the pentascale (5 note scale) with the right hand while the left hand plays a perfect harmonic (or blocked) 5th interval. We move up diatonically (according to the C major scale - i.e. C D E F G A B C). After doing one measure where the right hand plays the pentascale and the left hand plays the perfect harmonic (or blocked) 5th interval, the hands switch patterns and the left hand plays the pentascale while the right hand plays the perfect harmonic (or blocked) 5th interval). This continues moving up according to the C major scale. After perfecting this, you should try to play this in every key.

Pentascale Practice

In this exercise we are playing the pentascale (5 note scale - i.e. C D E F G) with the right hand while the left hand plays a perfect melodic (or broken) 5th interval (i.e. C - G). We move up diatonically (according to the C major scale - i.e. C D E F G A B C). After perfecting this exercise, you should try to play this in every key signature following the circle of 5ths.

5 1   Same fingering for both hands throughout the exercise.

All Major Pentascales

(following the circle of 5ths)

C major pentascale

same fingering in all keys (following the circle/cycle of fifths)

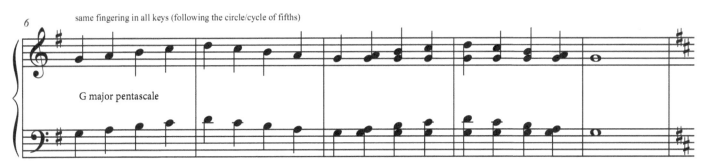

G major pentascale

same fingering in all keys (following the circle/cycle of fifths)

D major pentascale

A major pentascale

All Major Pentascales (following the circle of 5^{ths}) - page 2

E major pentascale

B major pentascale

C flat major pentascale

Enharmonics - B and C flat sound the same

F sharp major pentascale

G flat major pentascale

Enharmonics - F Sharp and G flat sound the same

C Sharp major pentascale

D Flat major pentascale

A Flat major pentascale

E Flat major pentascale

B Flat major pentascale

Enharmonics - C Sharp and D flat sound the same

F major pentascale

C major pentascale

All Minor Pentascales

(following the circle of 5ths)

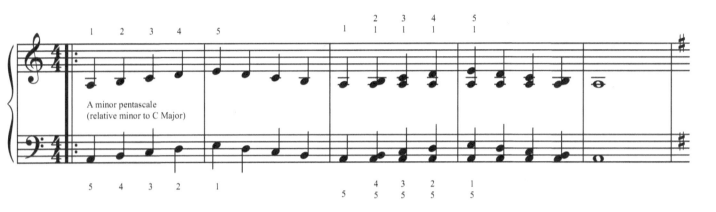

A minor pentascale
(relative minor to C Major)

same fingering in all keys (following the circle/cycle of fifths)

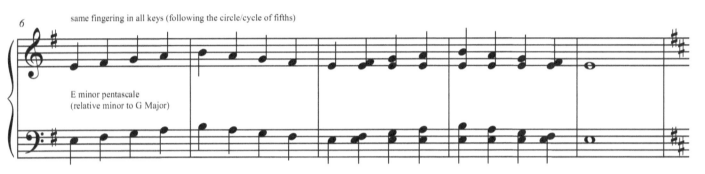

E minor pentascale
(relative minor to G Major)

same fingering in all keys (following the circle/cycle of fifths)

B minor pentascale
(relative minor to D Major)

F sharp minor pentascale
(relative minor to A Major)

All Minor Pentascales (following the circle of 5ths) - page 2

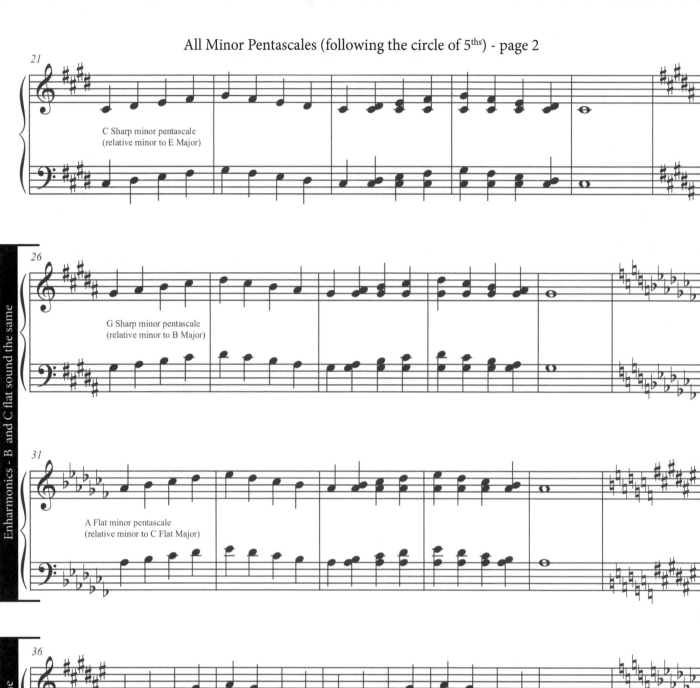

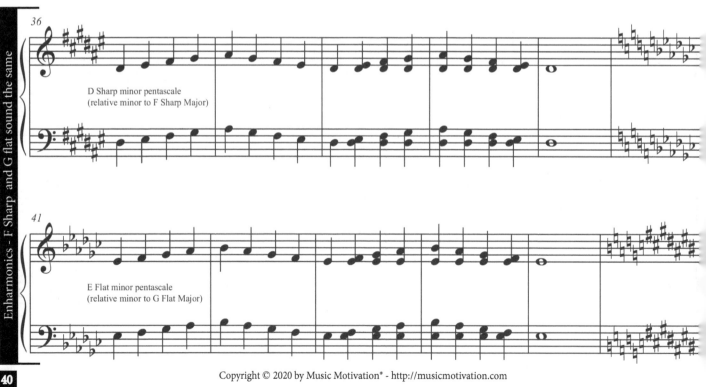

All Minor Pentascales (following the circle of 5ths) - page 3

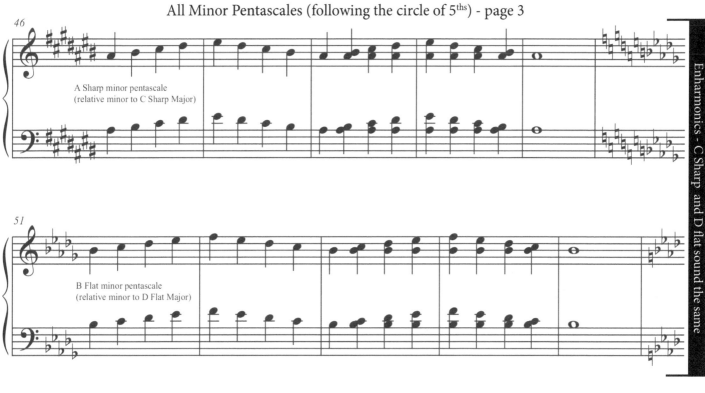

A Sharp minor pentascale
(relative minor to C Sharp Major)

B Flat minor pentascale
(relative minor to D Flat Major)

F minor pentascale
(relative minor to A Flat Major)

C minor pentascale
(relative minor to E Flat Major)

G minor pentascale
(relative minor to B Flat Major)

71

D minor pentascale
(relative minor to F Major)

76

A minor pentascale
(relative minor to C Major)

All Diminished Pentascales

(following the circle of 5ths)

A diminished pentascale

same fingering in all keys (following the circle/cycle of fifths)

E diminished pentascale

same fingering in all keys (following the circle/cycle of fifths)

B diminished pentascale

F ♯ diminished pentascale

Copyright © 2020 by Music Motivation® - http://musicmotivation.com

C♯ diminished pentascale

Enharmonics - B and C flat sound the same

G♯ diminished pentascale

A♭ diminished pentascale

Enharmonics - F Sharp and G flat sound the same

D♯ diminished pentascale

E♭ diminished pentascale

A♯ diminished pentascale

B♭ diminished pentascale

F diminished pentascale

C diminished pentascale

G diminished pentascale

Enharmonics - C Sharp and D flat sound the same

71

D diminished pentascale

76

A diminished pentascale

All Major Pentascales (eighth notes)

(following the circle of 5ths)

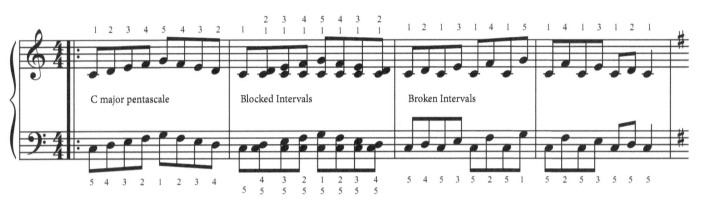

C major pentascale — Blocked Intervals — Broken Intervals

same fingering in all keys (following the circle/cycle of fifths)

G major pentascale

same fingering in all keys (following the circle/cycle of fifths)

D major pentascale

A major pentascale

All Major Pentascales - eighth notes (following the circle of 5ths) - page 2

C Sharp major pentascale

D Flat major pentascale

A Flat major pentascale

E Flat major pentascale

B Flat major pentascale

Enharmonics - C Sharp and D flat sound the same

All Minor Pentascales (eighth notes)

(following the circle of 5ths)

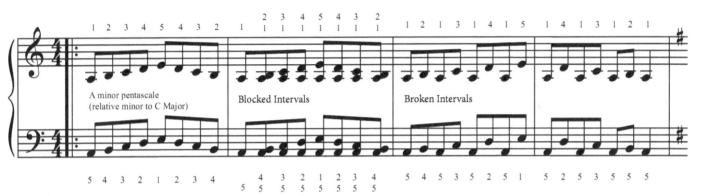

A minor pentascale
(relative minor to C Major)

Blocked Intervals

Broken Intervals

same fingering in all keys (following the circle/cycle of fifths)

E minor pentascale
(relative minor to G Major)

same fingering in all keys (following the circle/cycle of fifths)

B minor pentascale
(relative minor to D Major)

F sharp minor pentascale
(relative minor to A Major)

All Minor Pentascales - eighth notes (following the circle of 5ths) - page 2

C Sharp minor pentascale
(relative minor to E Major)

Enharmonics - B and C flat sound the same

G Sharp minor pentascale
(relative minor to B Major)

A Flat minor pentascale
(relative minor to C Flat Major)

Enharmonics - F Sharp and G flat sound the same

D Sharp minor pentascale
(relative minor to F Sharp Major)

E Flat minor pentascale
(relative minor to G Flat Major)

All Minor Pentascales - eighth notes (following the circle of 5ths) - page 3

A Sharp minor pentascale
(relative minor to C Sharp Major)

B Flat minor pentascale
(relative minor to D Flat Major)

F minor pentascale
(relative minor to A Flat Major)

C minor pentascale
(relative minor to E Flat Major)

G minor pentascale
(relative minor to B Flat Major)

D minor pentascale
(relative minor to F Major)

A minor pentascale
(relative minor to C Major)

All Diminished Pentascales (eighth notes)

(following the circle of 5ths)

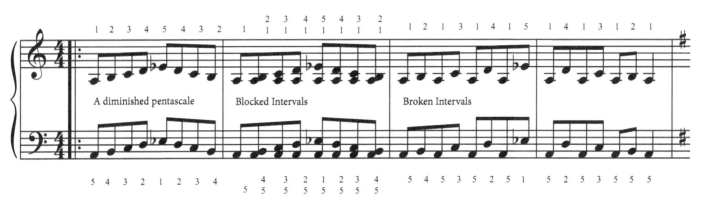

A diminished pentascale Blocked Intervals Broken Intervals

same fingering in all keys (following the circle/cycle of fifths)

E diminished pentascale

same fingering in all keys (following the circle/cycle of fifths)

B diminished pentascale

F# diminished pentascale

The "Maestro Stage" begins on page 68 and continues until page 165. The "Virtuoso Stage" begins on page 166 and continues until page 255.

Students are encouraged to take all of the suggested exercises, and once perfected, play them up and down the piano 1, 2, 3, and 4 octaves until the student feels confident and comfortable to do them memorized in all keys and without looking at the music.

	♪ Maestro ♪ for 2nd - 4th year students	♪ Virtuoso ♪ for 3rd year students and above
	Music Motivation® Book(s)	**Music Motivation® Book(s)**
	Essential Piano Exercises (section 2) An Introduction to Scales and Modes Cool Songs for Cool Kids (book 2) Cool Songs for Cool Kids (book 3) Variations on Mary Had a Little Lamb Twinkle Those Stars, Jazzed about Christmas, Jazzed about 4th of July Baroque, Romantic, Classical, Jazz, Blues, Popular, New Age, Student's Choice, Personal Composition.	Essential Piano Exercises (section 3) Cool Songs that ROCK! (books 1 & 2) Triumphant, Sea Fever, Sweet Melancholy, The Dawn of a New Age, Sweet Modality, Jazzed about Jazz, Jazzed about Classical Music, Jingle Those Bells, Cinematic Solos, Hymn Arranging Baroque, Romantic, Classical, Jazz, Blues, Popular, New Age, Contemporary, Broadway Show Tunes, Standards, Student's Choice, Personal Composition
Music Terminology	Tempo Markings Dynamic Markings Parts of the Piano Styles and Genres of Music *Music Motivation® 2nd Year Terminology*	Pocket Music Dictionary (2 - 3 years) Harvard Dictionary of Music (4 + years) Parts/History of the Piano Music Composers (Weekly Biographies) *Music Motivation® 3rd Year Terminology*
Key Signatures	Circle of 5ths/Circle of 4ths All Major and Minor key signatures (Identify each key and name the sharps and flats)	Spiral of Fifths, Chord Progressions within Key Signatures. Modulating from one Key Signature to another.
Music Notation	Names and Positions of notes above and below the staff (both hands)	History of Music Notation (the development of notation), Monks & Music, Gregorian Chants, Music changes over the years and how music has changed. Learn **Finale** and **Logic Pro** (notate your music)
Rhythms	Sixteenth notes/rests (say it and play it - count out loud) Thirty-second notes/rests (say it and play it - count out loud) Sixty-fourth notes/rests (say it and play it - count out loud)	One-hundred-twenty-eighth notes/rests For more on rhythm, I recommend: "Rhythmic Training" by Robert Starer and "Logical Approach to Rhythmic Notation" (books 1 & 2) by Phil Perkins
Intervals	All Perfect, Major, Minor, Augmented, and Diminished intervals (in every key) All Harmonic and Melodic intervals Explain the intervals used to create major, minor, diminished, and augmented chords?	9th, 11th, and 13th intervals Analyze music (Hymns and Classical) to identify intervals used in each measure. Identify/Name intervals used in chords.
Scales	All Major Scales (Every Key 1 - 2 octaves) All Minor Scales (Every Key 1 - 2 octaves) (natural, harmonic, and melodic minor scales) (Do, Di, Re, Ri, Mi, Fa, Fi, Sol, Si, La, Li, Ti, Do) (solfege - chromatic)	All Major Scales (Every Key 3 - 5 Octaves) All Minor Scales (Every Key 3 - 5 Octaves) All Blues Scales (major and minor) Cultural Scales (25 + scales)
Modes	All Modes (I, D, P, L, M, A, L) All keys	Modulating with the Modes (Dorian to Dorian)
Chords	All Major, Minor, Diminished, Augmented, Sus 2, Sus 4, Sixth, Minor Sixth, Dominant 7th and Major 7th Chords	Review All Chords from 1st and 2nd year experiences All 7th, 9th, 11th, and 13th chords inversions and voicings.
Arpeggios	Same chords as above (3 - 4 octaves)	Same chords as above (4 + octaves)
Inversions	Same chords as above (3 - 4 octaves)	Same chords as above (4 + octaves)
Technique	Wieck, Hanon, Bach (well tempered clavier)	Bertini-Germer, Czerny, I. Philipp
Sight Reading	Key of C, G, D, A, E, F, B♭, E♭, A♭, D♭	All Key Signatures, Hymns, Classical
Ear Training	C, D, E, F, G, A, B, and intervals	Key Signatures and Chords, Play w/ IPod
Music History	Baroque, Classical, Jazz, Blues	Students choice - All genres, Composers
Improvisation	Blues Pentascale, Barrelhouse Blues	Classical, New Age, Jazz, Blues, etc. Play w/ IPod
Composition	One - Two Page Song (include key change)	Lyrical, Classical, New Age, Jazz, etc.

This is the beginning of section two of this book. Section one primarily focused on exercises in pentascale position starting with C Major Pentascale (C D E F and G). After perfecting the C Major Pentascale students start playing all of the pentascales moving up according the C Major scale. Once students have been able to play all of the pentascales created from the notes of the C Major scale, they begin playing all of the Major, minor, and diminished pentascales in all key signatures following the circle of 5ths (i.e. C then G, D, A, E, B, etc.). When learning scales, it is easier to follow the circle of 5ths. When learning chords it is easier to move up chromatically or in half steps through every key signature. This helps the fingers learn muscle memory because the patterns of the chords are the same in key signature and the same fingering is used.

Now that we are starting section two of this book, we will be going over the following:

- Using Tetra Chords (learning what they are and how to create scales using them - page 61
- The degree names and scale degrees of each scale - page 64
- All Major Scales, Intervals, Triads, and Octave Chords - page 72
- All Minor Scales - page 132
- All Perfect 5th Intervals - page 140
- All Perfect Octave Intervals - page 141
- All Major Triads (root, 1st, and 2nd inversions) - page 142
- All Minor Triads (root, 1st, and 2nd inversions) - page 146
- All Diminished Triads (root, 1st, and 2nd inversions) - page 150
- All Augmented Triads (root, 1st, and 2nd inversions) - page 154
- All Sus4 Triads (root, 1st, and 2nd inversions) - page 158
- All Sus2 Triads (root, 1st, and 2nd inversions) - page 162
- All 6th Chords (root, 1st, 2nd, and 3rd inversions) - page 166
- All Minor 6th Chords (root, 1st, 2nd, and 3rd inversions) - page 170
- All Major 7th Chords (root, 1st, 2nd, and 3rd inversions) - page 174
- All Minor Major 7th Chords (root, 1st, 2nd, and 3rd inversions) - page 178
- All 7th Chords (Dominant) (root, 1st, 2nd, and 3rd inversions) - page 182
- All Minor 7th Chords (root, 1st, 2nd, and 3rd inversions) - page 186
- All Minor 7th Flat 5 Chords (root, 1st, 2nd, and 3rd inversions) - page 190
- All Minor 7th Sharp 5 Chords (root, 1st, 2nd, and 3rd inversions) - page 194
- All Diminished 7th Chords (root, 1st, 2nd, and 3rd inversions) - page 198
- Cadences (Plagal, Authentic, Complete Authentic) - page 205
- I - IV - V - V7 - I Chord Progressions - page 206
- I - IV - V - V7 - I Chord Progressions (inversions) - page 210
- i - iv - V - V7 - i Chord Progressions - page 214
- i - iv - V - V7 - i Chord Progressions (inversions) - page 218
- All Triads Built From the Major Scales - page 222
- All 7th Chords (moving up diatonically) - page 226
- Most Common Chords (in all keys) - page 230
- All Major Octave Chords (blocked and broken) - page 236
- The Practical Application of Music Theory - page 240
- Cool Songs by Jerald Simon (from the Cool Songs Series and the Cool Songs Club) - page 256
- Join the Essential Piano Exercises Course created by Jerald Simon - page 280

To begin playing scales we must examine the very basic steps for creating them. All scales are created from combining two tetrachords. The word "tetra" is Greek and means four. The word "chord" simply means a combination of two or more notes played together at the same time (as with harmonic chords - think harmony) or one right after the other at different times (as with melodic chords - think melody or arpeggio, which literally means broken chord).

A tetrachord must be four notes in alphabetical order (such as C, D, E and F) and follow a pattern of a whole step (the distance between the 1st and 2nd notes), another whole step (the distance between the 2nd and 3rd notes, and a half step (the distance between the 3rd and 4th notes). A half step is the distance from any black or white key to the very next key to the right (up above) or to the left (down below) with no key in between (i.e. C to C sharp). A whole step is equal to two half steps (i.e. C to D). This means there is a key on the piano in between the first and second notes. This is what the C tetrachord (C, D, E, and F) looks like in standard music notation:

This is the C tetrachord (C, D, E, and F)

Now take a look at the G tetrachord (G, A, B, and C) and notice how it follows the same rules: four notes in alphabetical order, with the pattern of a whole step, another whole step, then a half step. As a reminder, on the piano, the order of the notes or musical alphabet is A, B, C, D, E, F, and G, then the notes start over with A and follow the same pattern across the entire keyboard. This is what the G tetrachord (G, A, B, and C) looks like in standard music notation:

This is the G tetrachord (G, A, B, and C)

Tetrachords are used to create scales. A scale is nothing more than two tetrachords (a set of four notes plus another set of four notes) played one after the other. A scale begins and ends on the same letter and is named after it. For example, if we combined the C tetra chord (C, D, E, and F) with the G tetra chord (G, A, B, and C) and wrote it out letter by letter it would look like this: C D E F G A B C. Notice how it begins and ends on C. It is called the C major scale. The whole and half steps used to create any major scale are: W W H W W W H (whole step, whole step, half step, whole step, whole step, whole step, half step). An easy way to remember this is to say (and the best I've heard) is: We Walked Home When We Walked Home. The first letter of each of the words creates the W W H W W W H pattern. To see more whole and half step patterns used to create the modes, turn to page 22.

This is what the C major scale (C D E F G A B C) looks like in music:

On this page and the next page, I show you how two tetra chords are combined to create every major scale. Once you know how to create tetra chords, you can easily create any scale in any key signature. Remember, the pattern is whole step - whole step - half step to create each individual tetra chord. Look at the examples on this page and the next page to see the two tetra chords used to create these scales.

On both this page and the previous page, I have shown you tetrachords and spelled out the individual notes for each tetrachord and major scale. Notice how the major scales show the accompanying key signature while the tetra chord example only shows flats or sharps. It is important to begin thinking in terms of key signatures. You can refer to pages 8 and 9 of this book to learn more about the circle of 5ths. On the next several pages, we will follow the circle of fifths and introduce each scale, intervals, triads, 7th chords, and exercises following the major scales of each major key signature.

On the next several pages I have included charts that summarize the degree names, scale degrees (intervals), scale names, one octave fingering of the major scale, scale triads, and the accompanying Roman numerals for each of the chords (triads or three note chords) created from the major scales. I have tried to create this as a visual representation or quick reference sheet to help students see a summary for each individual key signature. I have found that when students can quickly identify the notes from each scale within a given key signature and they understand the progression of the chords built from the major scale, their piano playing ability improves overall. When students know this information, they sight-read better, their ability to move across the keys playing scales and chords improves, and they are also able to use this information to better help them improvise, create, and compose music of their own.

Below is an example of what this key signature reference guide looks like (this example is for the Key of C Major - on the next several pages a guide is included for every key signature following the circle of 5ths). I will now explain what everything means in this guide and how to use it in your piano playing.

✧ Key of C Major ✧

Degree Names	Tonic	Super Tonic	Mediant	Sub Dominant	Dominant	Sub Mediant	Leading Tone	Tonic
Scale Degrees (intervals)	1 P1	2 M2	3 M3	4 P4	5 P5	6 M6	7 M7	8 (1) P8 (octave)
Scale Names	C	D	E	F	G	A	B	C
One Octave (scale fingering)	rh 1 lh 5	2 4	3 3	1 2	2 1	3 3	4 2	5 1
Scale Triads	M	m	m	M	M	m	d	M
Roman Numerals	I	ii	iii	IV	V	vi	vii^{o}	VIII (I)

There are six horizontal rows. There are nine vertical columns. The first vertical column on the far left explains what is in each of the columns. The columns follow the major scale from left to right (i.e. C D E F G A B and C). Each of the nine vertical columns are matched up with or correspond with the first column categories. They are all listed from top to bottom as follows: 1. Degree Names, 2. Scale Degrees (intervals), 3. Scale Names, 4. One Octave (scale fingering), 5. Scale Triads, and 6. Roman Numerals. Let me explain what they mean.

The degree names refers to the name of each degree of the scale. It is listed: Tonic (i.e. C), Super Tonic (i.e. D), Mediant (i.e. E), Sub Dominant (i.e. F), Dominant (i.e. G), Sub Mediant (i.e. A), Leading Tone (i.e. B), and Tonic (i.e. C). The Scale Degrees (intervals) refers to the intervals from C. C is a prime or unison first interval, C to D is a major second interval (M2), C to E is a major third interval (M3), C to F is a perfect fourth interval (P4), C to G is a perfect fifth interval (P5), C to A is a major sixth interval (M6), C to B is a major seventh interval (M7), and C - C (one octave above) is an eighth interval (P8 - octave). The scale names represents each individual note found in the major scale (i.e. C D E F G A B C). The One Octave (scale fingering) shows the right hand (rh) and left hand (lh) fingerings for the notes from the scale (Scale Names). The Scale Triads is the same for every major scale: M m m M M m d M which means the triad/chord quality: Major triad (M), minor triad (m), minor triad (m), Major triad (M), Major triad (M), minor triad (m), diminished triad (d^{o}), Major triad (M). This is the chord progression created from each major scale. The Roman Numerals are upper case for Major chords and lower case for minor chords. The gray vertical columns represent Major chords - the white vertical columns are minor or diminished chords.

The gray columns are the primary chords and the white columns represent the secondary chords. It's a visual way to quickly identify the I - IV - V chords (primary - or major) versus the ii - iii - vi - vii chords.

❧ Key of C Major ❧

Degree Names	Tonic	Super Tonic	Mediant	Sub Dominant	Dominant	Sub Mediant	Leading Tone	Tonic
Scale Degrees (intervals)	1 P1	2 M2	3 M3	4 P4	5 P5	6 M6	7 M7	8 (1) P8 (octave)
Scale Names	C	D	E	F	G	A	B	C
One Octave (scale fingering)	rh 1 lh 5	2 4	3 3	1 2	2 1	3 3	4 2	5 1
Scale Triads	M	m	m	M	M	m	d	M
Roman Numerals	I	ii	iii	IV	V	vi	vii°	VIII (I)

❧ Key of G Major ❧

Degree Names	Tonic	Super Tonic	Mediant	Sub Dominant	Dominant	Sub Mediant	Leading Tone	Tonic
Scale Degrees (intervals)	1 P1	2 M2	3 M3	4 P4	5 P5	6 M6	7 M7	8 (1) P8 (octave)
Scale Names	G	A	B	C	D	E	F♯	G
One Octave (scale fingering)	rh 1 lh 5	2 4	3 3	1 2	2 1	3 3	4 2	5 1
Scale Triads	M	m	m	M	M	m	d	M
Roman Numerals	I	ii	iii	IV	V	vi	vii°	VIII (I)

❧ Key of D Major ❧

Degree Names	Tonic	Super Tonic	Mediant	Sub Dominant	Dominant	Sub Mediant	Leading Tone	Tonic
Scale Degrees (intervals)	1 P1	2 M2	3 M3	4 P4	5 P5	6 M6	7 M7	8 (1) P8 (octave)
Scale Names	D	E	F♯	G	A	B	C♯	D
One Octave (scale fingering)	rh 1 lh 5	2 4	3 3	1 2	2 1	3 3	4 2	5 1
Scale Triads	M	m	m	M	M	m	d	M
Roman Numerals	I	ii	iii	IV	V	vi	vii°	VIII (I)

Key of A Major

Degree Names	Tonic	Super Tonic	Mediant	Sub Dominant	Dominant	Sub Mediant	Leading Tone	Tonic
Scale Degrees (intervals)	1 P1	2 M2	3 M3	4 P4	5 P5	6 M6	7 M7	8 (1) P8 (octave)
Scale Names	A	B	C♯	D	E	F♯	G♯	A
One Octave (scale fingering)	rh 1 lh 5	2 4	3 3	1 2	2 1	3 3	4 2	5 1
Scale Triads	M	m	m	M	M	m	d	M
Roman Numerals	I	ii	iii	IV	V	vi	vii°	VIII (I)

Key of E Major

Degree Names	Tonic	Super Tonic	Mediant	Sub Dominant	Dominant	Sub Mediant	Leading Tone	Tonic
Scale Degrees (intervals)	1 P1	2 M2	3 M3	4 P4	5 P5	6 M6	7 M7	8 (1) P8 (octave)
Scale Names	E	F♯	G♯	A	B	C♯	D♯	E
One Octave (scale fingering)	rh 1 lh 5	2 4	3 3	1 2	2 1	3 3	4 2	5 1
Scale Triads	M	m	m	M	M	m	d	M
Roman Numerals	I	ii	iii	IV	V	vi	vii°	VIII (I)

Key of B Major

Degree Names	Tonic	Super Tonic	Mediant	Sub Dominant	Dominant	Sub Mediant	Leading Tone	Tonic
Scale Degrees (intervals)	1 P1	2 M2	3 M3	4 P4	5 P5	6 M6	7 M7	8 (1) P8 (octave)
Scale Names	B	C♯	D♯	E	F♯	G♯	A♯	B
One Octave (scale fingering)	rh 1 lh 4	2 3	3 2	1 1	2 4	3 3	4 2	5 1
Scale Triads	M	m	m	M	M	m	d	M
Roman Numerals	I	ii	iii	IV	V	vi	vii°	VIII (I)

Key of F Sharp Major

Degree Names	Tonic	Super Tonic	Mediant	Sub Dominant	Dominant	Sub Mediant	Leading Tone	Tonic
Scale Degrees (intervals)	1 P1	2 M2	3 M3	4 P4	5 P5	6 M6	7 M7	8 (1) P8 (octave)
Scale Names	F♯	G♯	A♯	B	C♯	D♯	E♯	F♯
One Octave (scale fingering)	rh 2 lh 4	3 3	4 2	1 1	2 3	3 2	1 1	2 4
Scale Triads	M	m	m	M	M	m	d	M
Roman Numerals	I	ii	iii	IV	V	vi	vii°	VIII (I)

Key of C Sharp Major

Degree Names	Tonic	Super Tonic	Mediant	Sub Dominant	Dominant	Sub Mediant	Leading Tone	Tonic
Scale Degrees (intervals)	1 P1	2 M2	3 M3	4 P4	5 P5	6 M6	7 M7	8 (1) P8 (octave)
Scale Names	C♯	D♯	E♯	F♯	G♯	A♯	B♯	C♯
One Octave (scale fingering)	rh 2 lh 3	3 2	1 1	2 4	3 3	4 2	1 1	2 3
Scale Triads	M	m	m	M	M	m	d	M
Roman Numerals	I	ii	iii	IV	V	vi	vii°	VIII (I)

On the next several pages I have included charts that summarize the degree names, scale degrees (intervals), scale names, one octave fingering of the major scale, scale triads, and the accompanying Roman numerals for each of the chords (triads or three note chords) created from the major scales for the key signatures using flats. Everything still applies and remains the same for the key signatures with flats.

One of the best ways to learn this material is to study these charts at the piano. You will be able to play the scales using the right and left hand fingering provided and can even memorize the order of the chord progression created from the Major scale (i.e. Major - minor - minor - Major - Major - minor - diminished - Major or M m m M M m d M). If you know how to play a C Major chord (tirad - C E and G played together at the same time), that is your starting chord for the key of C Major. From there, simply move those three notes to the right on the piano - only playing the white keys, until you arrive at the C Major chord an octave up to the right.

Key of F Major

Degree Names	Tonic	Super Tonic	Mediant	Sub Dominant	Dominant	Sub Mediant	Leading Tone	Tonic
Scale Degrees (intervals)	1 P1	2 M2	3 M3	4 P4	5 P5	6 M6	7 M7	8 (1) P8 (octave)
Scale Names	F	G	A	B♭	C	D	E	F
One Octave (scale fingering)	rh 1 lh 5	2 4	3 3	4 2	1 1	2 3	3 2	4 1
Scale Triads	M	m	m	M	M	m	d	M
Roman Numerals	I	ii	iii	IV	V	vi	vii°	VIII (I)

Key of B Flat Major

Degree Names	Tonic	Super Tonic	Mediant	Sub Dominant	Dominant	Sub Mediant	Leading Tone	Tonic
Scale Degrees (intervals)	1 P1	2 M2	3 M3	4 P4	5 P5	6 M6	7 M7	8 (1) P8 (octave)
Scale Names	B♭	C	D	E♭	F	G	A	B♭
One Octave (scale fingering)	rh 2(4) lh 3	1 2	2 1	3 4	1 3	2 2	3 1	4 3
Scale Triads	M	m	m	M	M	m	d	M
Roman Numerals	I	ii	iii	IV	V	vi	vii°	VIII (I)

Key of E Flat Major

Degree Names	Tonic	Super Tonic	Mediant	Sub Dominant	Dominant	Sub Mediant	Leading Tone	Tonic
Scale Degrees (intervals)	1 P1	2 M2	3 M3	4 P4	5 P5	6 M6	7 M7	8 (1) P8 (octave)
Scale Names	E♭	F	G	A♭	B♭	C	D	E♭
One Octave (scale fingering)	rh 3(2) lh 3	1 2	2 1	3 4	4 3	1 2	2 1	3(2) 3
Scale Triads	M	m	m	M	M	m	d	M
Roman Numerals	I	ii	iii	IV	V	vi	vii°	VIII (I)

Key of A Flat Major

Degree Names	Tonic	Super Tonic	Mediant	Sub Dominant	Dominant	Sub Mediant	Leading Tone	Tonic
Scale Degrees (intervals)	1 P1	2 M2	3 M3	4 P4	5 P5	6 M6	7 M7	8 (1) P8 (octave)
Scale Names	A♭	B♭	C	D♭	E♭	F	G	A♭
One Octave (scale fingering)	rh 2(3) lh 3	3(4) 2	1 1	2 4	3 3	1 2	2 1	3 3
Scale Triads	M	m	m	M	M	m	d	M
Roman Numerals	I	ii	iii	IV	V	vi	vii°	VIII (I)

Key of D Flat Major

Degree Names	Tonic	Super Tonic	Mediant	Sub Dominant	Dominant	Sub Mediant	Leading Tone	Tonic
Scale Degrees (intervals)	1 P1	2 M2	3 M3	4 P4	5 P5	6 M6	7 M7	8 (1) P8 (octave)
Scale Names	D♭	E♭	F	G♭	A♭	B♭	C	D♭
One Octave (scale fingering)	rh 2 lh 2(3)	3 2	1 1	2 4	3 3	4 2	1 1	2 3
Scale Triads	M	m	m	M	M	m	d	M
Roman Numerals	I	ii	iii	IV	V	vi	vii°	VIII (I)

Key of G Flat Major

Degree Names	Tonic	Super Tonic	Mediant	Sub Dominant	Dominant	Sub Mediant	Leading Tone	Tonic
Scale Degrees (intervals)	1 P1	2 M2	3 M3	4 P4	5 P5	6 M6	7 M7	8 (1) P8 (octave)
Scale Names	G♭	A♭	B♭	C♭	D♭	E♭	F	G♭
One Octave (scale fingering)	rh 2 lh 4	3 3	4 2	1 1	2 3	3 2	1 1	2 4
Scale Triads	M	m	m	M	M	m	d	M
Roman Numerals	I	ii	iii	IV	V	vi	vii°	VIII (I)

ꕤ Key of C Flat Major ꕤ

Degree Names	Tonic	Super Tonic	Mediant	Sub Dominant	Dominant	Sub Mediant	Leading Tone	Tonic
Scale Degrees (intervals)	1 P1	2 M2	3 M3	4 P4	5 P5	6 M6	7 M7	8 (1) P8 (octave)
Scale Names	C♭	D♭	E♭	F♭	G♭	A♭	B♭	C♭
One Octave (scale fingering)	rh 1 lh 4	2 3	3 2	1 1	2 4	3 3	4 2	1 1
Scale Triads	M	m	m	M	M	m	d	M
Roman Numerals	I	ii	iii	IV	V	vi	vii°	VIII (I)

On pages 72 - 101, I have created, what I feel, are essential piano exercises for every key signature. The exercises feature two pages worth of exercises in every key signature following the circle of fifths (i.e. C - G - D - A - E - B - F sharp - C sharp) first through key signatures with sharps, and then moving on to the key signatures with flats (i.e. F - B flat - E flat - A flat - D flat - G flat - C flat). I included the following exercises in every key signature:

- **One Octave Scales** (*contrary motion*)
- **One Octave Scales** (*parallel motion*)
- **Two Octave Scales** (*contrary motion*)
- **Two Octave Scales** (*parallel motion*)
- **Intervals** created from the major scale (*blocked and broken*)
- **Triads** (or three note chords) created from the major scale - Major, minor, minor, Major, Major, minor, diminished {dim.}, Major (i.e. C Maj., D min., E min., F Maj., G Maj., A min., B dim., C Maj.) - blocked and broken
- **Broken Triads** (perfect 5th interval {outside intervals} followed by the third)
- **Broken Triads** (third interval followed by the fifth)
- **Seventh chords** created from the major scale (Major 7th, minor 7th, minor 7th, Major 7th, dominant 7th, minor 7th, minor 7th flat 5, Major 7th - i.e. C Maj7, D min7, E min7, F Maj7, G7, A min7, B min7 flat 5, C Maj7)

After many years of teaching, giving workshops, seminars, master classes, and presentations for piano teaching groups, associations, and individual piano studios, and after having spoken with thousands of piano teachers and students around the world, I have found that students learn scales better following the circle of fifths. Jazz scales are best learned following the circle/cycle of 4ths. Ideally, a piano student should be able to play any scale in any key without relying on the circle of 5ths. When learning chords, however, students often do better moving up in half steps because of the patterns and fingering associated with chords that are similar in structure and quality (i.e. all major chords, or all minor sixth chords moving up in half steps etc.).

I did not include 3 or 4 octave scales because I feel once a student can successfully play two octave scales, they can figure out how to play three and four octaves scales as well. I don't think there is a need to notate three and four octave scales, however, I encourage piano players to practice each of these scales up and down the piano one, two, three, and four octaves (when applicable).

72

73

Key of C Octave chords created from the C Major Scale (blocked and broken chords moving up and down diatonically.

74

Simple bass note while the right hand plays the I - IV - V - V7 - I Chord Progression

Practical real world application...

76

Key of G Octave chords created from the G Major Scale (blocked and broken chords moving up and down diatonically.

78

One Octave Scales

D Major Scale (contrary motion - 1 octave)   D Major Scale (parallel motion - 1 octave)

Two Octave Scales (contrary and parallel motion)

D Major Scale (contrary motion - 2 octaves)

D Major Scale (parallel motion - 2 octaves)

Key of D Intervals

1st 2nd 3rd 4th 5th 6th 7th 8th

Key of D TRIADS

D   Em   F#m   G   A   Bm   C#dim   D   D   C#dim   Bm   A

same fingering with every chord (both hands)

Key of D Octave chords created from the D Major Scale (blocked and broken chords moving up and down diatonically.

E Major Scale (contrary motion - 1 octave)   E Major Scale (parallel motion - 1 octave)

E Major Scale (contrary motion - 2 octaves)

E Major Scale (parallel motion - 2 octaves)

1st 2nd 3rd 4th 5th 6th 7th 8th

E   F#m   G#m   A   B   C#m   D#dim   E   E   D#dim   C#m   B

same fingering with every chord (both hands)

One Octave Scales

Two Octave Scales (contrary and parallel motion)

Key of E Intervals

Key of E TRIADS

One Octave Scales

B Major Scale (contrary motion - 1 octave)   B Major Scale (parallel motion - 1 octave)

Two Octave Scales (contrary and parallel motion)

B Major Scale (contrary motion - 2 octaves)

B Major Scale (parallel motion - 2 octaves)

(G#) (A#) (B)

Key of B Intervals

1st 2nd 3rd 4th 5th 6th 7th 8th

Key of B TRIADS

B   C#m D#m   E   F#   G#m A#dim B   B   A#dim   G#m   F#

same fingering with every chord (both hands)

Key of B Major - Octave chords created from the B Major Scale (blocked and broken chords moving up and down diatonically.

Key of F Sharp Major – Octave chords created from F Sharp Major Scale (blocked and broken chords moving up and down diatonically.

98

C sharp Major Scale (contrary motion - 1 octave)

C sharp Major Scale (parallel motion - 1 octave)

One Octave Scales

C sharp Major Scale (contrary motion - 2 octaves)

C sharp Major Scale (parallel motion - 2 octaves)

Two Octave Scales (contrary and parallel motion)

Key of C Sharp Intervals

1st 2nd 3rd 4th 5th 6th 7th 8th

Key of C Sharp TRIADS

C# D#m F m F# G# A#m C dim C#   C#   C dim   A#m   G#

same fingering with every chord (both hands)

Key of C Sharp - Broken Triads (three note chords)

Key of C Sharp - 7th Chords (blocked and broken)

102

Key of C Sharp Major - Octave chords created from C Sharp Major Scale (blocked and broken chords moving up and down diatonically.

F Major Scale (contrary motion - 1 octave)

F Major Scale (parallel motion - 1 octave)

One Octave Scales

Two Octave Scales (contrary and parallel motion)

F Major Scale (contrary motion - 2 octaves)

F Major Scale (parallel motion - 2 octaves)

Key of F - Intervals

1st 2nd 3rd 4th 5th 6th 7th 8th

Key of F - TRIADS

F   Gm   Am   B♭   C   Dm   E dim   F   F   E dim   Dm   C

same fingering with every chord (both hands)

Key of F Major - Octave chords created from the F Major Scale (blocked and broken chords moving up and down diatonically.

B Flat Major Scale (contrary motion - 1 octave)

B Flat Major Scale (parallel motion - 1 octave)

B Flat Major Scale (contrary motion - 2 octaves)

B Flat Major Scale (parallel motion - 2 octaves)

1st 2nd 3rd 4th 5th 6th 7th 8th

B♭ Cm Dm E♭ F Gm A dim B♭   B♭   A dim   G m   F

same fingering with every chord (both hands)

One Octave Scales

Two Octave Scales (contrary and parallel motion)

Key of B Flat - Intervals

Key of B Flat - TRIADS

109

Simple bass note while the right hand plays the I - IV - V - V7 - I Chord Progression

Practical real world application...

One Octave Scales

E Flat Major Scale (contrary motion - 1 octave)   E Flat Major Scale (parallel motion - 1 octave)

Two Octave Scales (contrary and parallel motion)

E Flat Major Scale (contrary motion - 2 octaves)

E Flat Major Scale (parallel motion - 2 octaves)

Key of E Flat - Intervals

1st 2nd 3rd 4th 5th 6th 7th 8th

Key of E Flat - TRIADS

E♭ Fm Gm A♭ B♭ Cm Ddim E♭   E♭   Ddim   Cm   B♭

same fingering with every chord (both hands)

Copyright © 2020 by Music Motivation® - http://musicmotivation.com

114

Primary Cadence

Primary Cadence (variation)

Simple bass note while the right hand plays the I - IV - V - V7 - I Chord Progression

Practical real world application...

One Octave Scales

A Flat Major Scale (contrary motion - 1 octave) A Flat Major Scale (parallel motion - 1 octave)

Two Octave Scales (contrary and parallel motion)

A Flat Major Scale (contrary motion - 2 octaves)

A Flat Major Scale (parallel motion - 2 octaves)

Key of A Flat - Intervals

1st 2nd 3rd 4th 5th 6th 7th 8th

Key of A Flat - TRIADS

A♭ B♭m C m D♭ E♭ F m G dim A♭ A♭ G dim F m E♭

same fingering with every chord (both hands)

116

117

Simple bass note while the right hand plays the I - IV - V - V7 - I Chord Progression

Practical real world application...

One Octave Scales

D Flat Major Scale (contrary motion - 1 octave)   D Flat Major Scale (parallel motion - 1 octave)

Two Octave Scales (contrary and parallel motion)

D Flat Major Scale (contrary motion - 2 octaves)

D Flat Major Scale (parallel motion - 2 octaves)

Key of D Flat - Intervals

1st 2nd 3rd 4th 5th 6th 7th 8th

Key of D Flat - TRIADS

D♭ E♭m F m G♭ A♭ B♭m C dim D♭ D♭ C dim B♭m A♭

same fingering with every chord (both hands)

120

Key of D Flat Major - Octave chords created from the D Flat Major Scale (blocked and broken chords moving up and down diatonically.

G Flat Major Scale (contrary motion - 1 octave)

G Flat Major Scale (parallel motion - 1 octave)

G Flat Major Scale (contrary motion - 2 octaves)

G Flat Major Scale (parallel motion - 2 octaves)

1st 2nd 3rd 4th 5th 6th 7th 8th

Gb Abm Bbm B   Db Ebm F dim Gb   Gb   F dim   Ebm   Db

same fingering with every chord (both hands)

Key of G Flat Major - Octave chords created from the G Flat Major Scale (blocked and broken chords moving up and down diatonically.

Simple bass note while the right hand plays the I - IV - V - V7 - I Chord Progression

Practical real world application...

127

C Flat Major Scale (contrary motion - 1 octave)

C Flat Major Scale (parallel motion - 1 octave)

C Flat Major Scale (contrary motion - 2 octaves)

C Flat Major Scale (parallel motion - 2 octaves)

1st 2nd 3rd 4th 5th 6th 7th 8th

Cb   Dbm   Ebm   Fb   Gb   Abm   Bbdim   Cb   Cb   Bbdim   Abm   Gb

One Octave Scales

Two Octave Scales (contrary and parallel motion)

Key of C Flat - Intervals

Key of C Flat - TRIADS

same fingering with every chord (both hands)

Simple bass note while the right hand plays the I - IV - V - V7 - I Chord Progression

Practical real world application...

Every major key signature has a relative minor key that is in the same key signature. The relative minor begins on the 6th degree (sub mediant) of the major scale. I refer to this as the happy and sad relatives. In the key of C major, C major is the happy relative. Going from C - C creates the C major scale. The 6th note above C is A. A minor is the relative minor of C major. A minor is always sad. Going from A - A (using only the white keys from the C major scale) creates the A minor scale.

There are three kinds of minor scales: the Natural (which is simply the relative minor), the Harmonic, and the Melodic. The harmonic is the most used minor scale of the three. Because of that, the scale triads are created from the harmonic minor scale. Below you will find a chart of the minor key signature triads (created from the harmonic minor scale). On the following pages you will play all of the minor scales (in all keys). The harmonic scale has a rasied seventh ascending and descending, and the melodic minor has a rasied sixth and seventh ascending, and lowered sixth and seventh when descending.

Minor Key Signatures

Degree Names	Tonic	Super Tonic	Mediant	Sub Dominant	Dominant	Sub Mediant	Leading Tone	Tonic
Scale Degrees (intervals)	1	2	3	4	5	6	7	8 (1)
Scale Triads	m	d°	Aug+	m	M	M	d°	m
Roman Numerals	i	ii°	III+	iv	V	VI	vii°	viii (i)
fingering for the (triads created from the) **Harmonic Minor Scales**	lh 1 3 5 / rh 5 3 1	lh 1 3 5 / rh 5 3 1	lh 1 3 5 / rh 5 3 1	lh 1 3 5 / rh 5 3 1	lh 1 3 5 / rh 5 3 1	lh 5 3 1 / rh 5 3 1	lh 5 3 1 / rh 5 3 1	lh 5 3 1 / rh 5 3 1
a 0	A	B	C	D	E	F	G♯	A
e 1	E	F♯	G	A	B	C	D♯	E
b 2	B	C♯	D	E	F♯	G	A♯	B
f♯ 3	F♯	G♯	A	B	C♯	D	E♯	F♯
c♯ 4	C♯	D♯	E	F♯	G♯	A	B♯	C♯
g♯ 5	G♯	A♯	B	C♯	D♯	E	F✕	G♯
d♯ 6	D♯	E♯	F♯	G♯	A♯	B	C✕	D♯
a♯ 7	A♯	B♯	C♯	D♯	E♯	F♯	G✕	A♯
fingering for the (triads created from the) **Harmonic Minor Scales**	lh 1 3 5 / rh 5 3 1	lh 1 3 5 / rh 5 3 1	lh 1 3 5 / rh 5 3 1	lh 1 3 5 / rh 5 3 1	lh 1 3 5 / rh 5 3 1	lh 5 3 1 / rh 5 3 1	lh 5 3 1 / rh 5 3 1	lh 5 3 1 / rh 5 3 1
a 0	A	B	C	D	E	F	G♯	A
d 1	D	E	F	G	A	B♭	C♯	D
g 2	G	A	B♭	C	D	E♭	F♯	G
c 3	C	D	E♭	F	G	A♭	B	C
f 4	F	G	A♭	B♭	C	D♭	E	F
b♭ 5	B♭	C	D♭	E♭	F	G♭	A	B♭
e♭ 6	E♭	F	G♭	A♭	B♭	C♭	D	E♭
a♭ 7	A♭	B♭	C♭	D♭	E♭	F♭	G	A♭

132

The letters in the chart represent chords (i.e. A minor, B diminished, C augmented, D minor, etc., according to the Harmonic minor scale. You can also read the individual letters moving from left to right as the individual notes from the scale in addition to up and down for chords.

Minor Scales

A minor Scale (natural)

A minor Scale (harmonic)

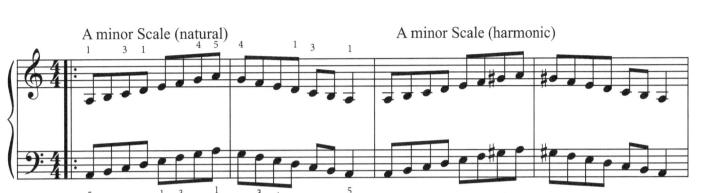

A minor Scale (melodic)

E minor Scale (natural)

E minor Scale (harmonic)

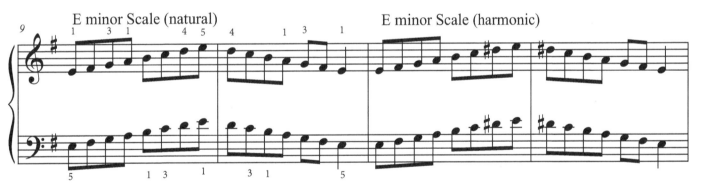

E minor Scale (melodic)

C sharp minor Scale (melodic)

G sharp minor Scale (natural)   G sharp minor Scale (harmonic)

G sharp minor Scale (melodic)

A flat minor Scale (natural)   A flat minor Scale (harmonic)

A flat minor Scale (melodic)

A sharp minor Scale (melodic)

B flat minor Scale (natural)   B flat minor Scale (harmonic)

B flat minor Scale (melodic)

F minor Scale (natural)   F minor Scale (harmonic)

F minor Scale (melodic)

A minor Scale (natural)   A minor Scale (harmonic)

A minor Scale (melodic)

All Perfect 5th Intervals

(moving up chromatically in half steps)

All Octave Intervals

(moving up chromatically in half steps)

All Major Triads (root, first, and second inversions)

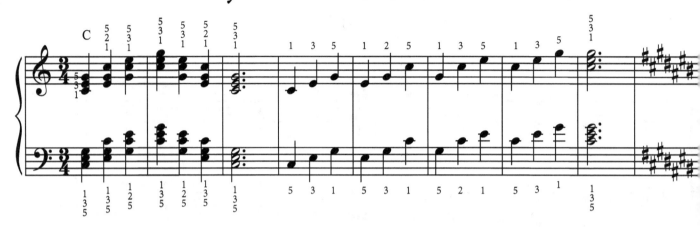

same fingering in all keys moving up chromatically (in half steps)

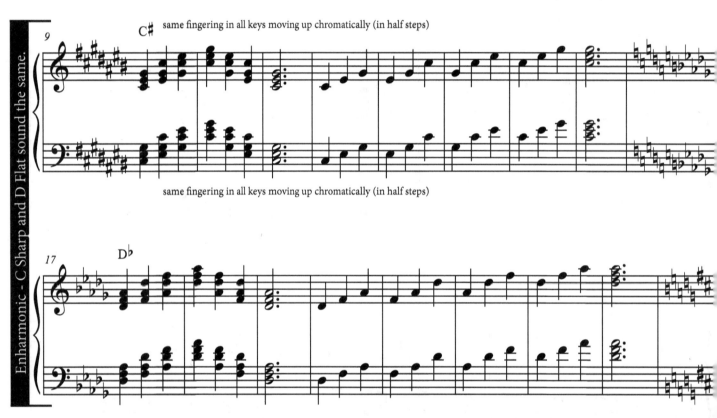

same fingering in all keys moving up chromatically (in half steps)

Enharmonic - C Sharp and D Flat sound the same.

In addition to playing this exercise as it is written, you should try to play all of the chords as arpeggios, or broken chords, up and down the piano one, two, three, and four octaves - in all key signatures.

Enharmonic - F Sharp and G Flat sound the same.

Copyright © 2020 by Music Motivation® - http://musicmotivation.com

143

All Minor Triads (root, first, and second inversions)

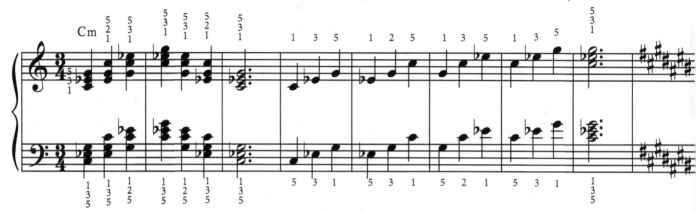

same fingering in all keys moving up chromatically (in half steps)

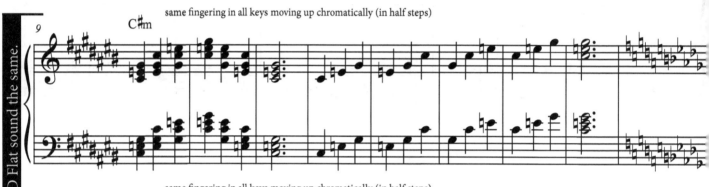

same fingering in all keys moving up chromatically (in half steps)

In addition to playing this exercise as it is written, you should try to play all of the chords as arpeggios, or broken chords, up and down the piano one, two, three, and four octaves - in all key signatures.

Enharmonic - F Sharp and G Flat sound the same

B and C Flat sound the same.

149

All Diminished Triads (root, first, and second inversions)

The ° symbol means a diminished chord. Sometimes the diminished chord is referred to as a minor flat 5 chord.

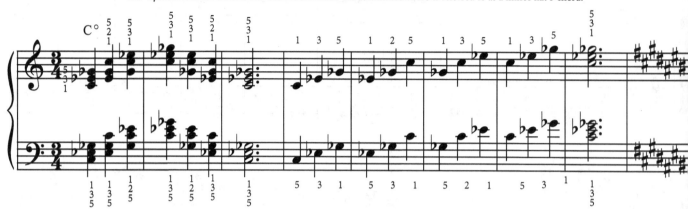

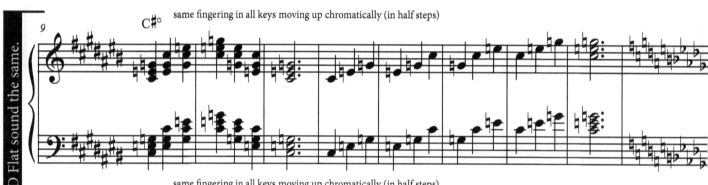

same fingering in all keys moving up chromatically (in half steps)

same fingering in all keys moving up chromatically (in half steps)

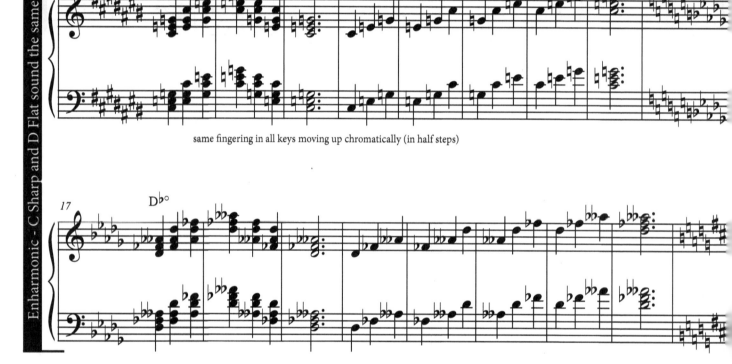

Enharmonic - C Sharp and D Flat sound the same.

In addition to playing this exercise as it is written, you should try to play all of the chords as arpeggios, or broken chords, up and down the piano one, two, three, and four octaves - in all key signatures.

Enharmonic - F Sharp and G Flat sound the same.

B and C Flat sound the same.

All Augmented Triads (root, first, and second inversions)

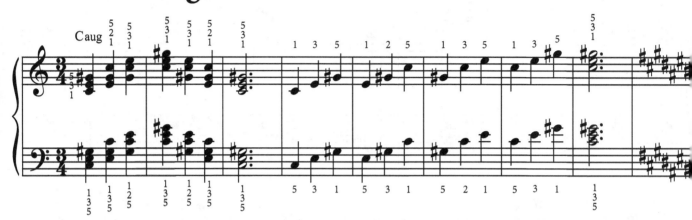

same fingering in all keys moving up chromatically (in half steps)

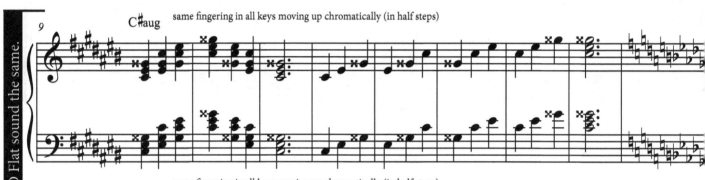

same fingering in all keys moving up chromatically (in half steps)

In addition to playing this exercise as it is written, you should try to play all of the chords as arpeggios, or broken chords, up and down the piano one, two, three, and four octaves - in all key signatures.

Enharmonic – F Sharp and G Flat sound the same.

155

156

All Sus4 Triads (root, first, and second inversions)

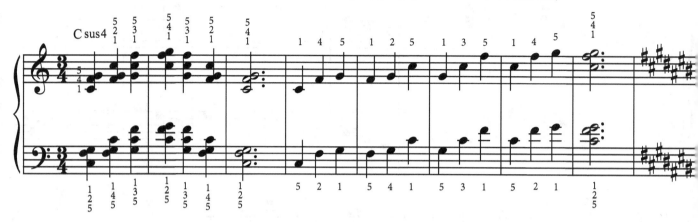

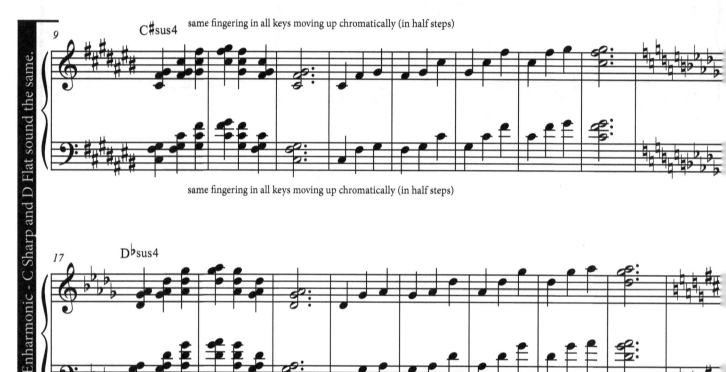

same fingering in all keys moving up chromatically (in half steps)

same fingering in all keys moving up chromatically (in half steps)

Enharmonic - C Sharp and D Flat sound the same.

In addition to playing this exercise as it is written, you should try to play all of the chords as arpeggios, or broken chords, up and down the piano one, two, three, and four octaves - in all key signatures.

159

Enharmonic - F Sharp and G Flat sound the same.

160

B and C Flat sound the same.

All Sus2 Triads (root, first, and second inversions)

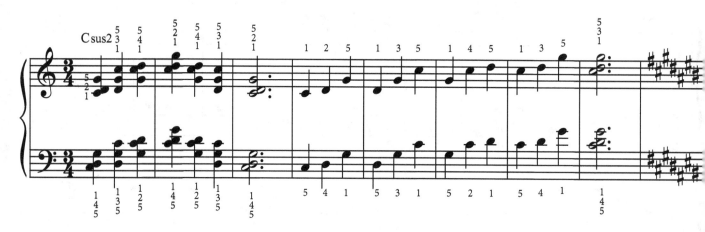

same fingering in all keys moving up chromatically (in half steps)

Enharmonic - C Sharp and D Flat sound the same.

In addition to playing this exercise as it is written, you should try to play all of the chords as arpeggios, or broken chords, up and down the piano one, two, three, and four octaves - in all key signatures.

Enharmonic - F Sharp and G Flat sound the same.

All 6th Chords (root, first, second, and third inversions)

Enharmonic - C Sharp and D Flat sound the same.

same fingering in all keys moving up chromatically (in half steps)

same fingering in all keys moving up chromatically (in half steps)

In addition to playing this exercise as it is written, you should try to play all of the chords as arpeggios, or broken chords, up and down the piano one, two, three, and four octaves - in all key signatures.

All Minor 6th Chords (root, first, second, and third inversions)

Enharmonic – C Sharp and D Flat sound the same.

same fingering in all keys moving up chromatically (in half steps)

same fingering in all keys moving up chromatically (in half steps)

In addition to playing this exercise as it is written, you should try to play all of the chords as arpeggios, or broken chords, up and down the piano one, two, three, and four octaves - in all key signatures.

171

172

All Major 7th Chords (root, first, second, and third inversions)

In addition to playing this exercise as it is written, you should try to play all of the chords as arpeggios, or broken chords, up and down the piano one, two, three, and four octaves - in all key signatures.

175

176

B and C Flat sound the same.

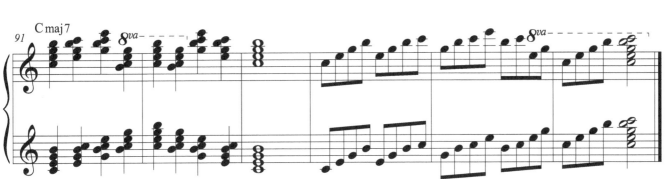

All Minor Major 7th Chords (root, first, second, and third inversions)

In addition to playing this exercise as it is written, you should try to play all of the chords as arpeggios, or broken chords, up and down the piano one, two, three, and four octaves - in all key signatures.

Enharmonic - F Sharp and G Flat sound the same.

All 7th Chords - Dominant (root, first, second, and third inversions)

In addition to playing this exercise as it is written, you should try to play all of the chords as arpeggios, or broken chords, up and down the piano one, two, three, and four octaves - in all key signatures.

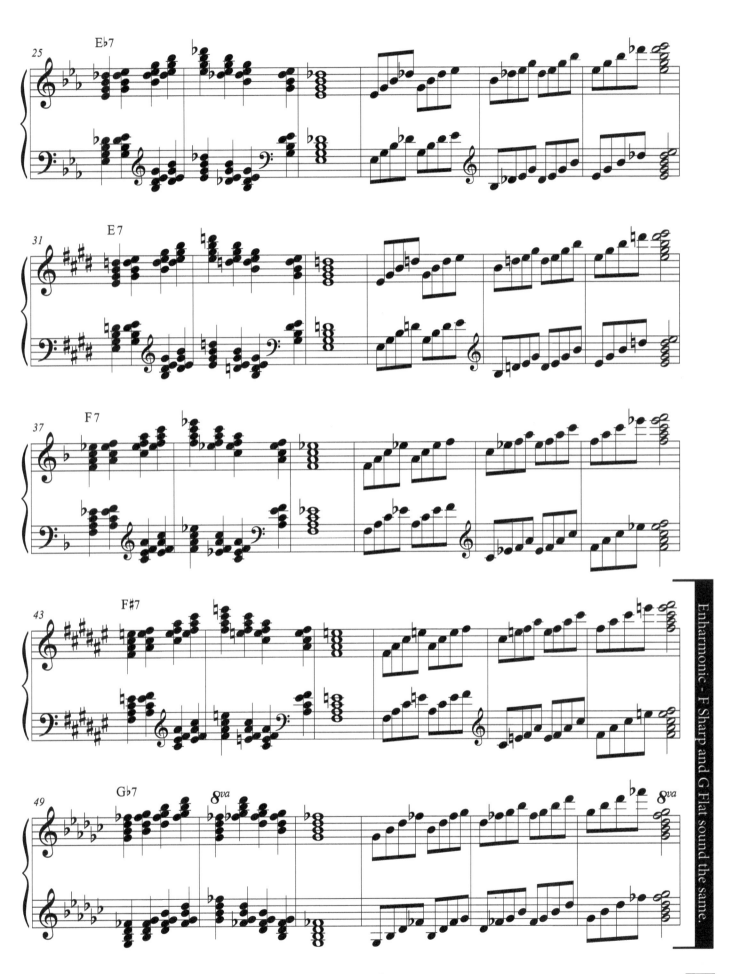

All Minor 7th Chords (root, first, second, and third inversions)

In addition to playing this exercise as it is written, you should try to play all of the chords as arpeggios, or broken chords, up and down the piano one, two, three, and four octaves - in all key signatures.

187

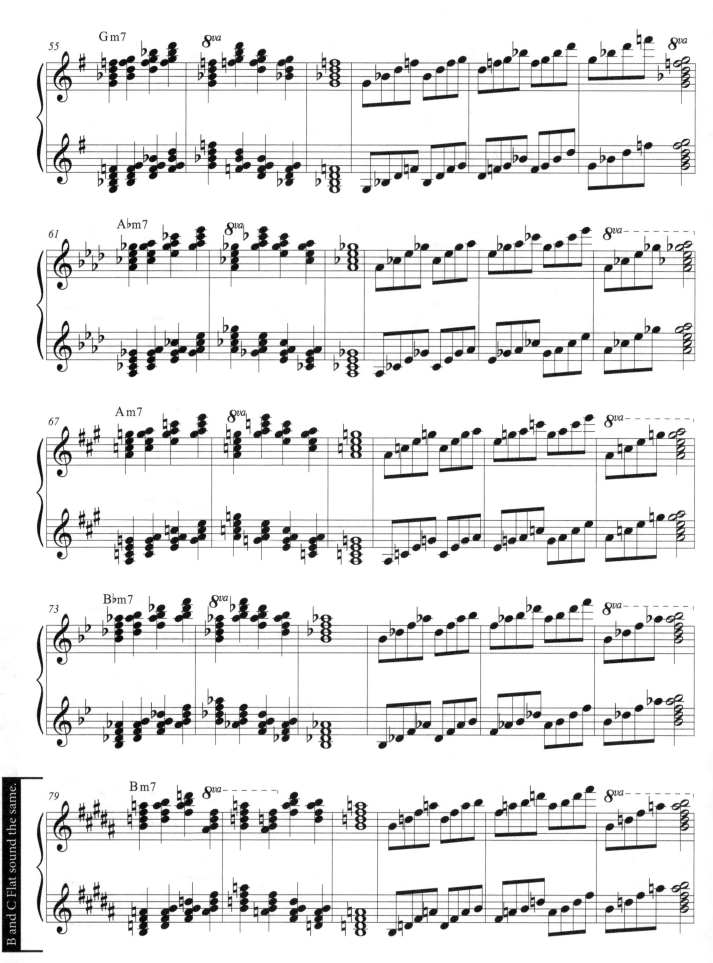

B and C Flat sound the same.

All Minor 7 Flat 5 Chords (root, first, second, and third inversions)

In addition to playing this exercise as it is written, you should try to play all of the chords as arpeggios, or broken chords, up and down the piano one, two, three, and four octaves - in all key signatures.

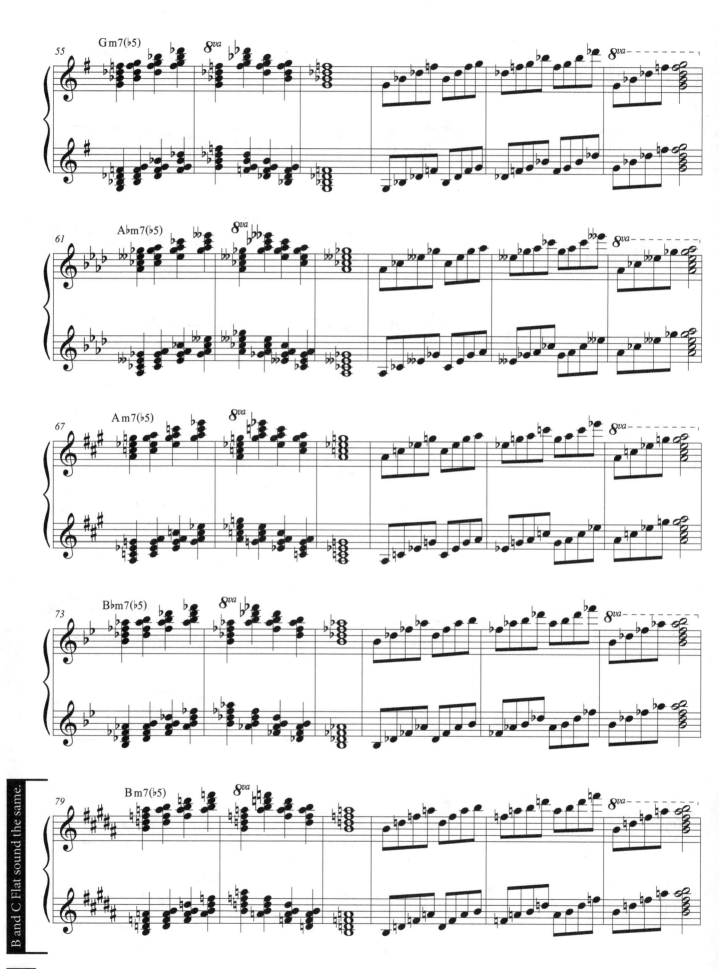

All Minor 7th Sharp 5 Chords (root, first, second, and third inversions)

In addition to playing this exercise as it is written, you should try to play all of the chords as arpeggios, or broken chords, up and down the piano one, two, three, and four octaves - in all key signatures.

Enharmonic - F Sharp and G Flat sound the same.

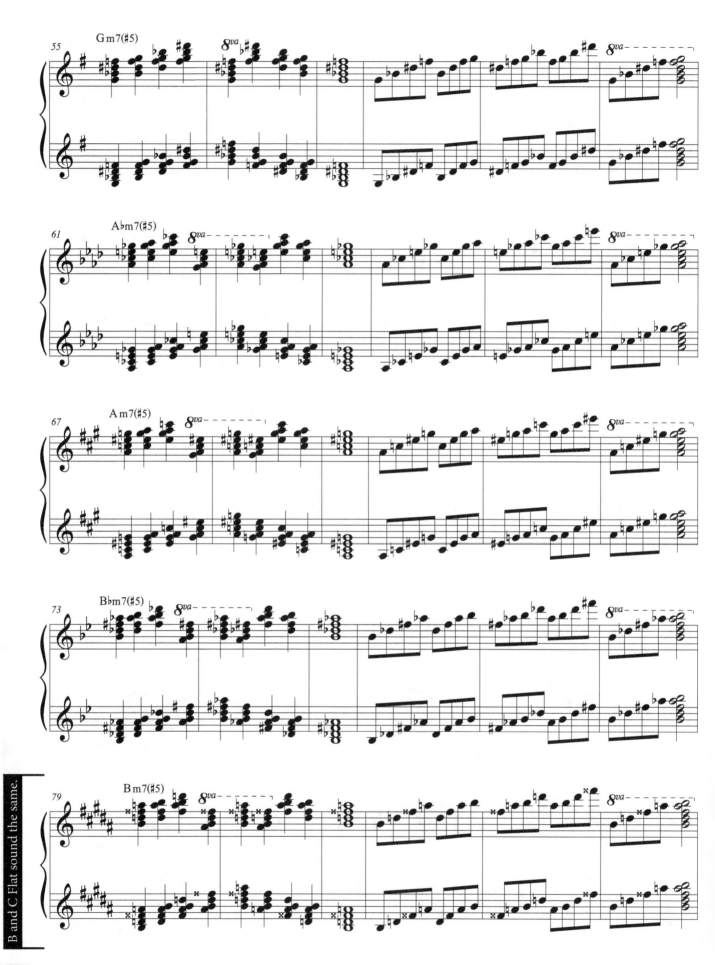

B and C Flat sound the same.

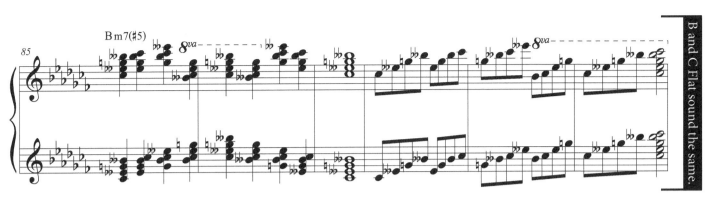

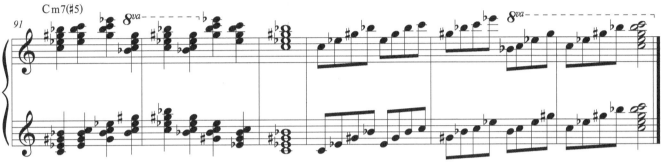

197

All Diminished 7th Chords (root, first, second, and third inversions)

In addition to playing this exercise as it is written, you should try to play all of the chords as arpeggios, or broken chords, up and down the piano one, two, three, and four octaves - in all key signatures.

199

C dim7

On the following pages (pages 204 - 221), I have included the "I-IV-V-V7-I" chord progression in all keys. These Roman numerals are taken from the degree of the scale notes (refer to pages 48-62 of this book for the details about the roman numerals or chord created from the scale shown as Roman numerals based on their position in the scale - e.g. I - ii - iii - IV - V - vi - vii - VIII or I (upper case Roman numerals are major chords and the lower case Roman numerals are minor chords with exception to the vii (7) chord which is a diminished triad).

Music books often speak of Cadences which are essentially chord progressions. Let me explain a few and then I'll explain why I chose the "I-IV-V-V7-I" chord progression to have the students practice in all keys.

Plagal Cadence (IV - I) or 4 - 1 (e.g. F to C)

The Plagal Cadence is a chord progression that moves from the IV (or 4 chord - e.g. F), and then returns to the I (or 1 chord - e.g. C). It would look like this: F - C. The chords can be played in any position (root, first, or second inversions), which simply means that the notes change position (e.g. root = CEG, first inversion = EGC where the C has been removed from the bottom of the chord and added to the top of the chord - basically inverting the notes of the chord, and second inversion = GCE where the C and the E have been removed from the bottom of the chord and added to the top of the chord.

Authentic Cadence (V - I) or 5 - 1 (the 5^7 is also used - e.g. G to C or G^7 to C)

The Authentic Cadence is a chord progression that moves from the V or V^7 (or 5 chord - e.g. G or G^7), and then returns to the I (or 1 chord - e.g. C). The same explanation about the inversions is correct.

Complete Authentic Cadence (I - IV - I - V7 - I) or 1 - 4 - 1 - 5^7 - 1

The Complete Authentic Cadence is a chord progression that moves from the I (or 1 chord - e.g. C), to the IV (or 4 chord - e.g. F), and then returns to the I (or 1 chord - e.g. C) and then plays the V7 (or 5 chord - e.g. G^7) before finally returning to the I (or 1 chord - e.g. C). This is the chord progression that is taught to music students and is traditionally the one they learn for various testings (AIM, Federation, MTNA, etc.). Students should learn how to do all of these cadences and many more in all keys and in all inversions. Look at the **Plagal Cadence**, **Authentic Cadence**, and **Complete Authentic Cadence** examples below:

Chord changes in contemporary music (or modern music of today) is more free in its form and structure, so I have included the I - IV - V - V^7 - I (e.g. C - F - G - G^7 - C) chord progression in all keys and in all inversions to better help students quickly change from the IV to the V chord as that is a familiar chord progression in modern music without first returning to the I chord as in the I - IV - I - V7 - I chord progression.

Have fun learning and mastering this chord progression in all keys - major and minor - and in all inversions!

I - IV - V - V7 - I Chord Progression (in every key signature)

(simple - Root - 2nd - 1st - 1st - Root - moving up chromatically in half steps)

same fingering in all keys moving up chromatically (in half steps)

same fingering in all keys moving up chromatically (in half steps)

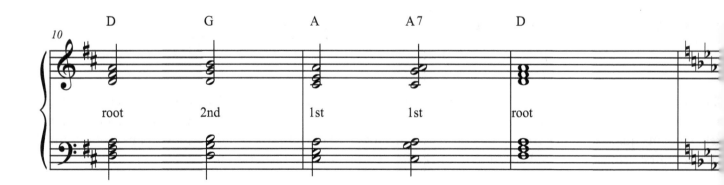

Enharmonic - C Sharp and D Flat sound the same.

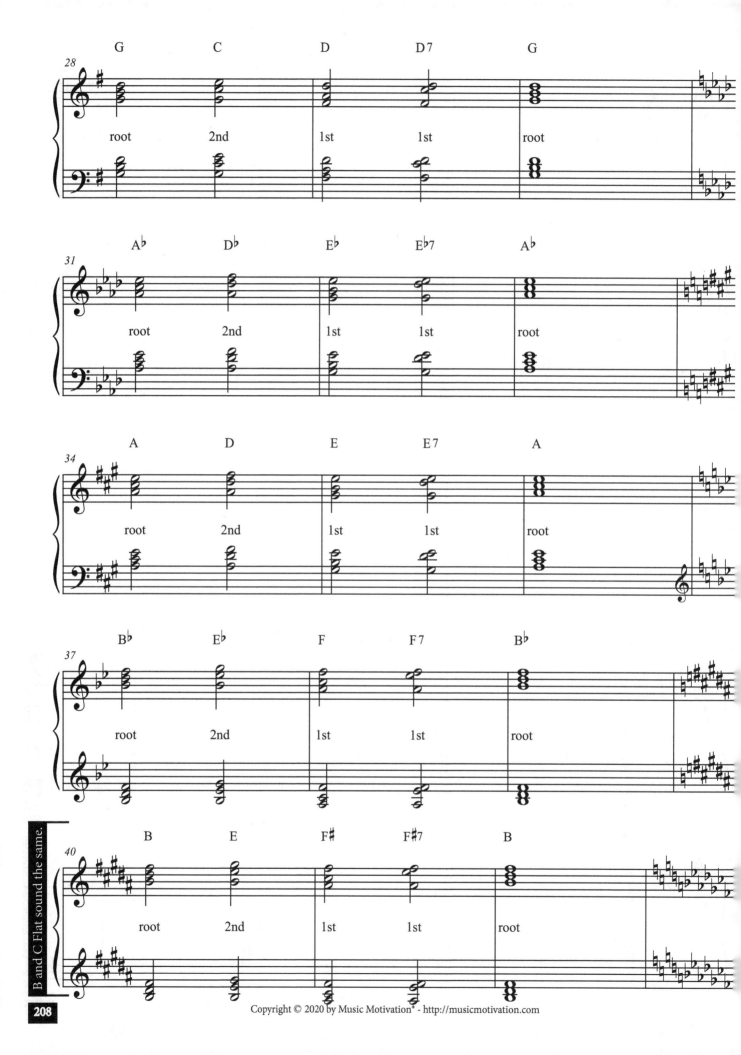

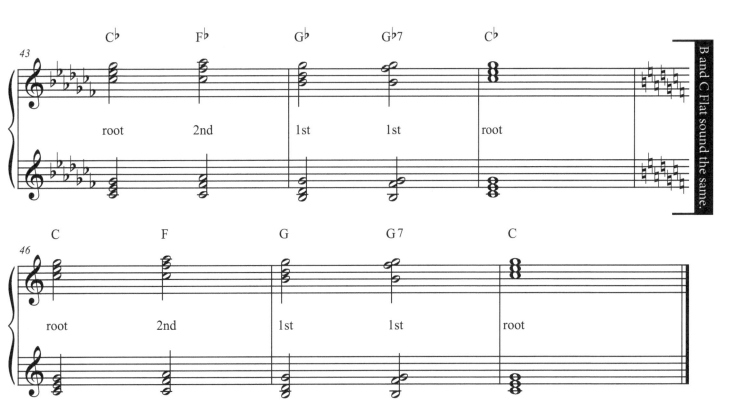

I - IV - V - V7 - I Chord Progression (in every key signature)

(complete - root, first, and second inversions in all keys - moving up chromatically in half steps)

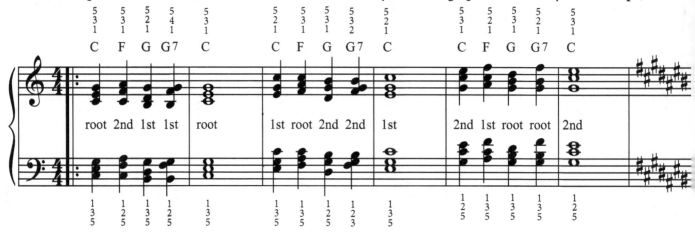

same fingering in all keys moving up chromatically (in half steps)

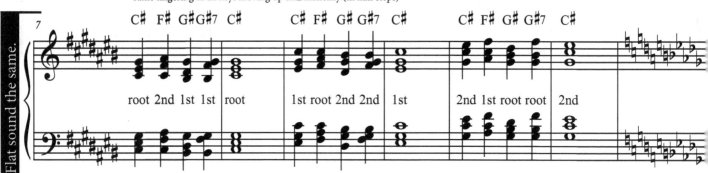

same fingering in all keys moving up chromatically (in half steps)

Enharmonic – C Sharp and D Flat sound the same.

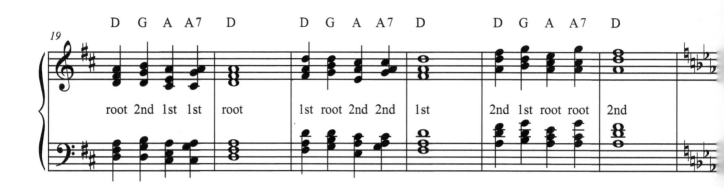

212

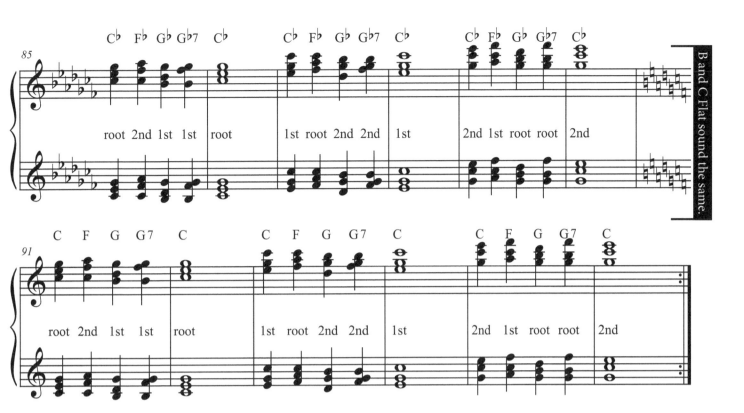

i - iv - V - V7 - i Chord Progression (in every key signature)

(simple - Root - 2nd - 1st - 1st - Root - moving up chromatically in half steps)

same fingering in all keys moving up chromatically (in half steps)

same fingering in all keys moving up chromatically (in half steps)

Enharmonic - C Sharp and D Flat sound the same.

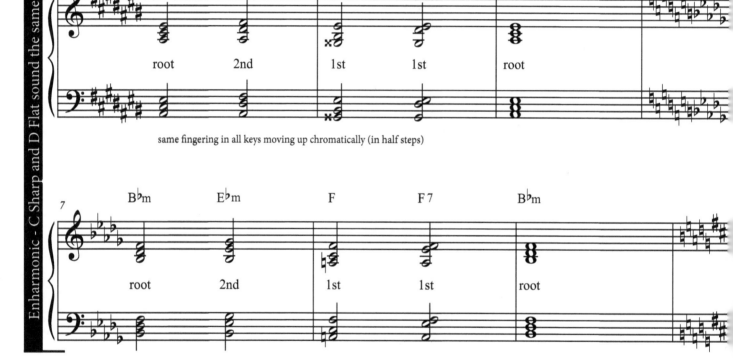

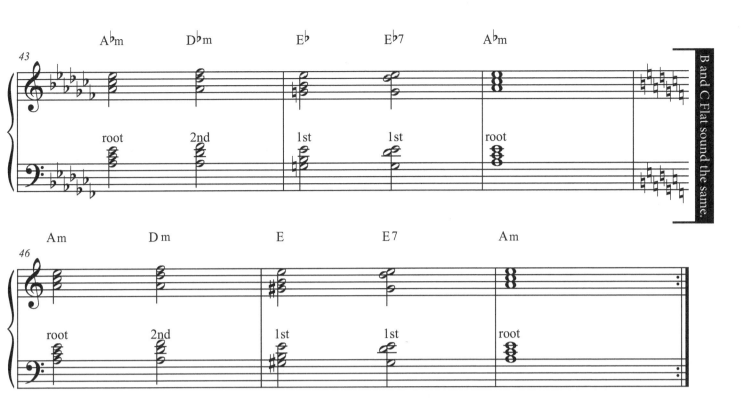

i - iv - V - V7 - i Chord Progression (in every key signature)

(complete - root, first, and second inversions in all keys - moving up chromatically in half steps)

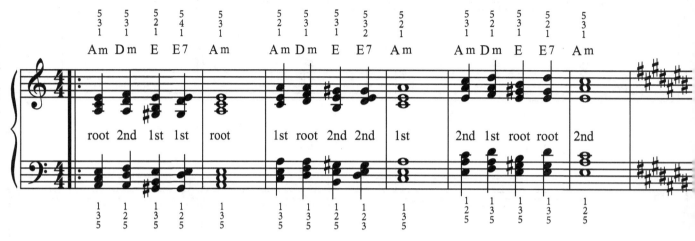

same fingering in all keys moving up chromatically (in half steps)

same fingering in all keys moving up chromatically (in half steps)

Enharmonic - C Sharp and D Flat sound the same.

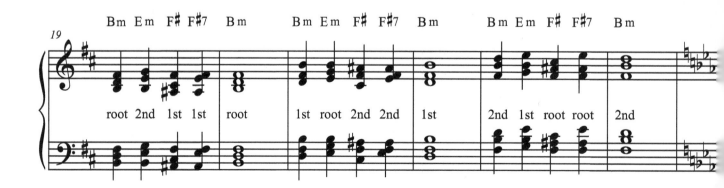

All Triads Built from the Major Scales

(following the Circle of 5ths through every key signature)

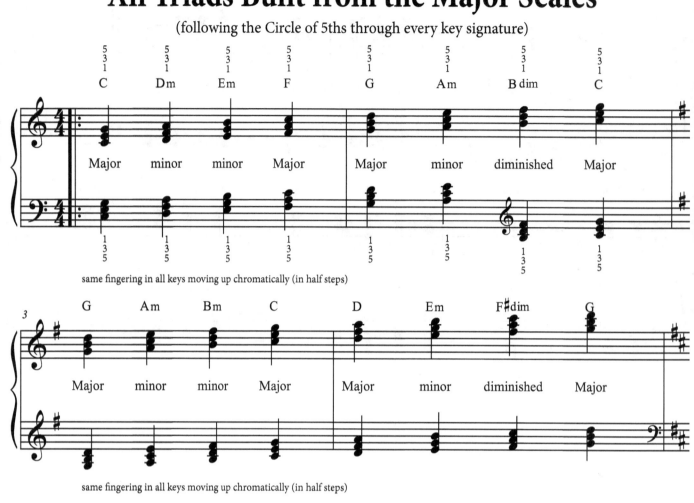

same fingering in all keys moving up chromatically (in half steps)

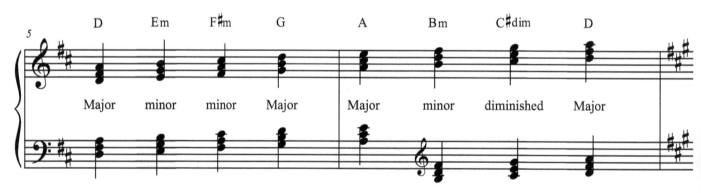

same fingering in all keys moving up chromatically (in half steps)

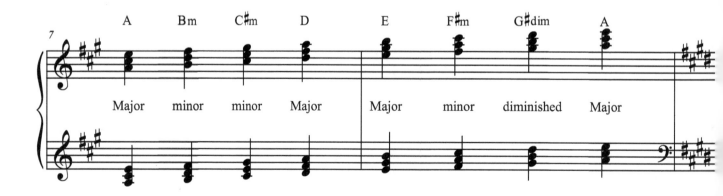

223

224

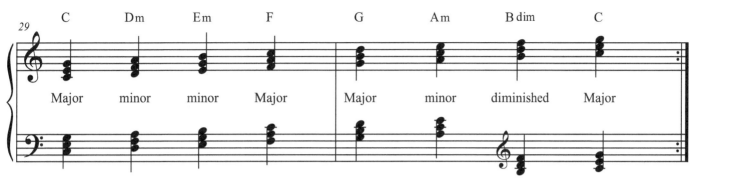

225

All 7th Chords (moving up diatonically)

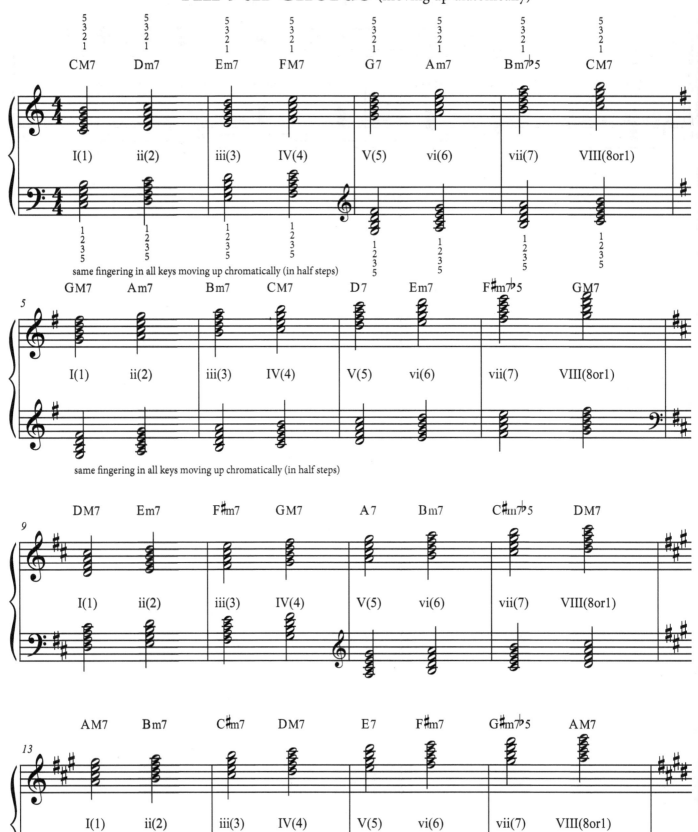

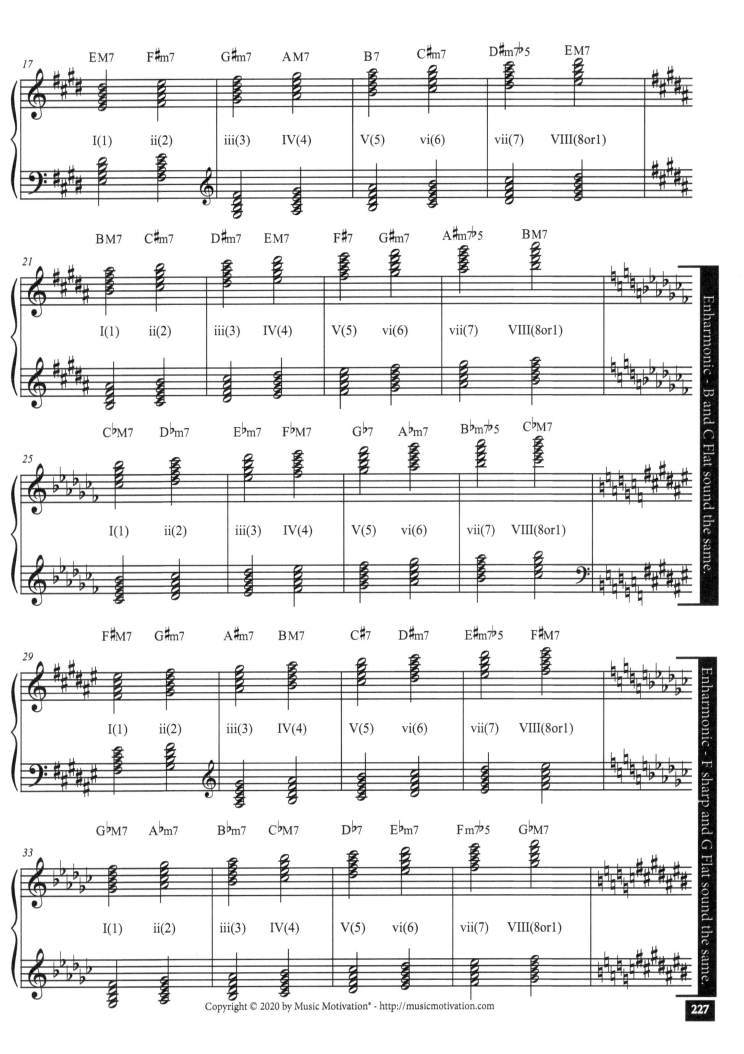

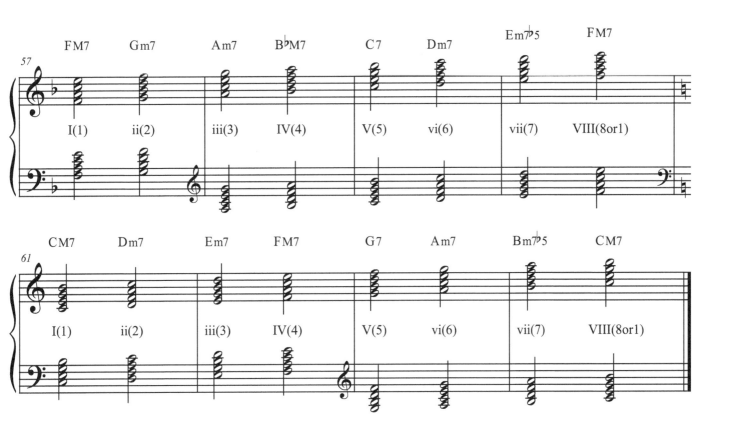

Most Common Chords (in all keys)

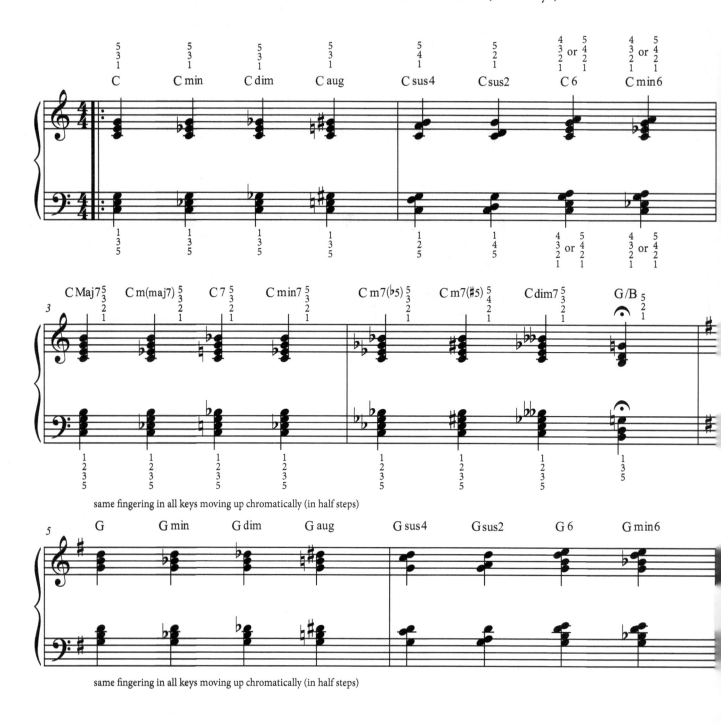

same fingering in all keys moving up chromatically (in half steps)

same fingering in all keys moving up chromatically (in half steps)

233

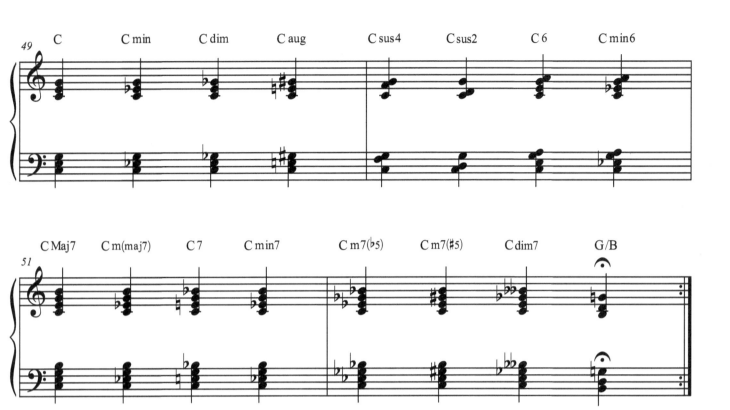

All Major Octave Chords (blocked and broken)

Moving up chromatically in half steps through every key signature

same fingering both hands in all keys moving up chromatically (in half steps)

same fingering both hands in all keys moving up chromatically (in half steps)

My Mission: (*My Primary Music Motivation® Goal*): Create fun, original piano music that is cool, exciting, entertaining, and educational to help motivate and inspire piano students! (especially teenage boys)!

My Music Motivation® Goal (for music educators): One of my primary goals at Music Motivation® is to help prepare the next generation of composers, arrangers, musicians, music teachers, and musicologists to use their music and their love of music to make a difference in their own lives, their community, and the world.

Music Motivation® is dedicated to motivating music students of all ages with "Music that excites, entertains, and educates"™. The three main areas of focus for Music Motivation® are: Theory Therapy™, Innovative Improvisation™, and Creative Composition™.

The Practical Application (of music theory)

Once you know the theory (i.e. intervals, scales, chords, etc.,) you need to know what to do with them!

The next 15 pages will contain exercises that are putting the music theory from the previous exercises into practice so you can see how to use intervals, chords, and scales in your own playing. First you need to learn the music theory (I call it Mental Memory - get the knowledge into your head), and then you need to actually incorporate it into your playing (I call it Muscle Memory - get the knowledge from your head to your hands).

Most of the following exercises are only notated in the key of C Major, but as with all of the other exercises in this thi book, I encourage you to play these in every key signature and inversion. Once you learn the music theory, you need to know what to do with it. There are many music theory books that teach music theory beautifully, but they never show you what to do with that knowledge. Other books show you great licks, patterns, progressions, and musical ideas, but don't explain the theory behind it. I hope in this book you will get both and will see how I am using the intervals, chords, and scales in creating music.

Sometimes, I think, we forget that songs are composed using music theory. Yes, there are musical motifs, as well as melodic and harmonic lines, and we need to know what we are doing, but we need to feel the music and let it become part of us. This goes beyond the notes on the page or the theory we read about analyzing structures and compound chords. It's about feeling, emotion, connecting with the music, and ultimately connecting with others those create music, and those who listen to the music we create. I hope I can show you some examples of how to use the exercises from the previous pages and create music of your own in the process. Let's get started and have some fun!

First let's talk about melodic and harmonic intervals (blocked and broken intervals - i.e. C - G - one played after the other and C and G played at the same time). Melodic intervals are played one after another while Harmonic intervals are played together at the same time. Earlier exercises in this book demonstrate how to play both blocked (harmonic) and broken (melodic) intervals. On the next few pages, see if you can identify the harmonic or melodic intervals in these exercises. Try to make up exercises of your own as well!

Here's a simple composition I created to demonstrate. Notice that my left hand is playing a perfect 5th harmonic interval (since C and G are played together at the same time this is a perfect 5th harmonic interval - with harmonic think of "harmony" or two notes played together at the same time). A simple way to think of the harmonic interval is to describe it as being blocked - notes played together at the same time (instead of melodic which is broken or one note played after another). My right hand is just playing around with the notes from the C Major Pentascale you played on pages 15 - 38.

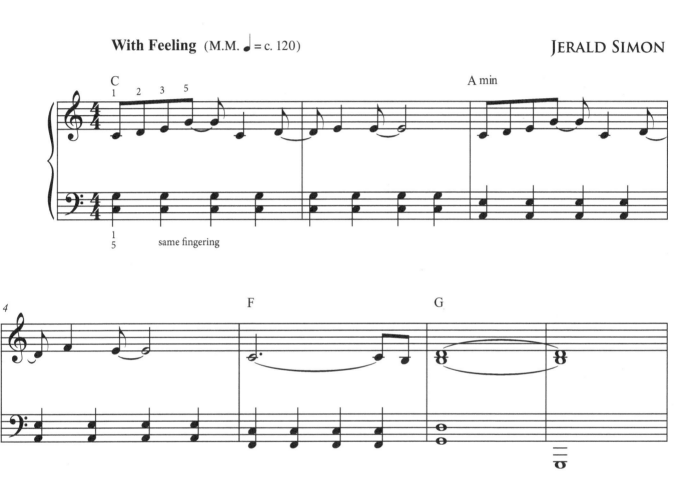

If you look at the chord progression, we start on C and then move to A minor, followed by F major and ending with G major. This chord progression is the I - vi - IV - V chord progression. You can play this exact progression in any key signature. Since we are in the key of C major, C is our I chord. If we were in the key of D major then D would be our I chord. The same is true if we were in the key of F sharp major. F sharp major would be the I chord. For fun, try playing this example in every key signature moving up in half steps. I did not write this out in every key signature because it is important to learn how to transpose something without having it written down in front of you. In fact, this entire section is primarily in the key of C Major. I have done this intentionally to help you work on changing the key signature without the music. Work on this and see what you can do. Feel free to complete this partial composition I composed. If you do, please film yourself playing this and share it with me. You can share it in my COOL SONGS Club Facebook group page at facebook.com/group/coolsongsclub.

On this page let's try to create a simple composition using the melodic (or broken) perfect 5th interval. Here's a simple composition I created to demonstrate this. Notice that my left hand is playing a perfect 5th melodic interval (since C and G are not played together at the same time, or one note after another, this is a perfect 5th melodic interval). Again, my right hand is just playing around with the notes from the C Major Pentascale you played on pages 15 - 38. Try to play this and then play around with it and see if you can compose something like this of your own. As with the previous example, try to play this short composition demonstration in all key signatures (moving up in half steps).

On the next few pages I have included some fun piano exercises that will help you practice these left hand melodic patterns with a major pentascale pattern/melody I created. I hope you enjoy these. After you perfect them as written, try to play them in every key signature moving up in half steps.

Techno-Pop Feel (♩ = c. 120)

JERALD SIMON

Same fingering for both hands throughout the exercise.

We are simply moving up the C Major scale - C D E F G A B and C playing all pentascales with the right hand starting on each of the steps of the C Major scale. The left hand moves up according to the C Major scale playin octave intervals. This is a great exercise to play around with and see what you can compose on your own. Just play any random notes with the right hand in any order and any rhythm while the left hand continues to play the octave interval. You can follow any chord progression you'd like. Try starting on C and then go to G, F, A, or any key signature of your choice and see what you can create!

Below is a simple composition I composed to demonstrate how to play the melodic octave interval (i.e. C and C) with the left hand while the right hand plays around with the notes from the C Major pentascale. I created this with somewhat of a techno-pop quality and feeling about it. Try to play this as it is written and then try to play this in every key signature moving up in half steps.

Let's try composing or improvising with chords. Throughout this book you have worked on learning you triads (three note chords - major, minor, diminished, augmented, Sus4, Sus2), your 6th and 7th chords (i.e. C6, C minor 6, C Maj 7, C minor Maj 7, C7, C minor 7, C minor 7 flat 5, C minor 7 sharp 5, C diminished 7 and so on). Before we start showing examples of chords, let's try to play all Major chords moving up in half steps and playing around rhythmically with the chords.

Here is an example of a simple chord progression: I - iii - IV - V (or C - E minor - F Major - G Major). In this example I play the blocked chord with my left hand and play the broken chord with my right hand and then I switch.

Here is an example of a simple I - IV - vi - V chord progression. Both hands are playing the I-IV-vi-V chord progression. The left hand is playing a 1 - 5 - 8 left hand pattern (i.e. C - G - C). Essentially it is a broken C Major Octave chord without the E note. The first page has everything written out. The second page has the left hand but the right hand has intentionally been left blank so you can improvise and create a melody of your own. Try it!

Here is an example of what you can do with octave chords. It's a simple demonstration of how you can compose something using octave chords (sometimes leaving out one of the four notes from the octave chord if you want to). Try playing this as it is and then in all key signatures! I did not add any fingering or dynamics because I would like to have you play this how you feel it should sound.

In addition to learning all chords in every inversion (i.e. root position, 1st, 2nd, and 3rd inversions), you should also be able to play all chords as arpeggios (or broken chords) up and down the piano. On the next two pages I have included the C6, Cm6, CMaj7, CmMaj7, C7, Cm7, Cm7 flat 5, Cm7 sharp 5, and the C diminished 7th chords played as arpeggios or broken chords up and down two octaves. After mastering two octaves on the piano, you should try to play the same exercises 2, 3, and 4 octaves up and down the piano.

The C6, Cm6, CMaj7, CmMaj7, C7, Cm7, Cm7 flat 5, Cm7 sharp 5, and the C diminished 7th chords played as arpeggios or broken chords up and down two octaves. Try playing these in every key! Once you have mastered these in the key of C, try playing all of these broken (arpeggiated) chords in every key signature moving up in half steps through every key signature 2, 3, and 4 octaves up and down the piano.

same fingering in all keys moving up chromatically (in half steps)

same fingering in all keys moving up chromatically (in half steps)

I love composing music using music theory and do it to help piano students understand how to apply music theory and why we learn these intervals, scales, and chords. I want students to understand how important it is and why they should learn and understand music theory in the first place. Instead of showing various examples, I thought I would include in this book 12 original compositions I have composed that are part of my COOL SONGS Series. I have created hundreds of piano pieces that have become known as COOL SONGS because many students who played these pieces said they sounded "COOL" and couldn't wait to play more. I have composed hundreds of these COOL SONGS complete with accompaniment MP3 minus tracks (guitars, keyboard synths, drums, bass, strings, etc.). It's fun for the piano students to learn music theory through these COOL SONGS and perform them at recitals, concerts, school talent shows, or for family and friends. You can learn more about these COOL SONGS on my website at: https://www.musicmotivation.com/coolsongs. You can even download a FREE 130 page PDF book I wrote on motivating piano students the FUN way (20 Ways to Motivate Teen Piano Students to Want to Play the Piano - the FUN Way!) It contains several of these COOL SONGS. Visit: https://www.musicmotivation.com/optin

The next several pages contain 12 FREE COOL SONGS I have composed that I am sharing as a COOL SONGS Starter Bundle in this book. Look for the theory. Notice the intervals, scales, chords (blocked and broken) that I incorporate into the music. The most important aspect is to have fun playing these COOL SONGS. I have not included the MP3 accompaniment minus tracks as part of this book, but if you download the FREE 130 page PDF book mentioned above (20 Ways to Motivate Teen Piano Students to Want to Play the Piano - the Fun Way!) I'll send you the MP3s so you can play along with the sheet music. Have fun with these!

Beginning Level COOL SONGS:

ATTACK!
Dolphins Play Every Day
The Gamer
Party

Early Intermediate Level COOL SONGS:

The A minor ACE
Sonic
Good Times
Spook

Intermediate to Advanced Level COOL SONGS:

When Sharks ATTACK!
Hybrid Hero
The Labyrinth
Boulevard

youtube.com/jeraldsimon
facebook.com/jeraldsimon

Jerald Simon
musicmotivation.com

Skill - We are in the key of C Major. This is a pre-primer/primer level piece for brand new students - especially younger students who are learning the note names. Have FUN playing this "Cool Song"!

Pre-Primer
or Primer
Level

Take No Prisoners (M.M. ♩ = c. 120)   JERALD SIMON

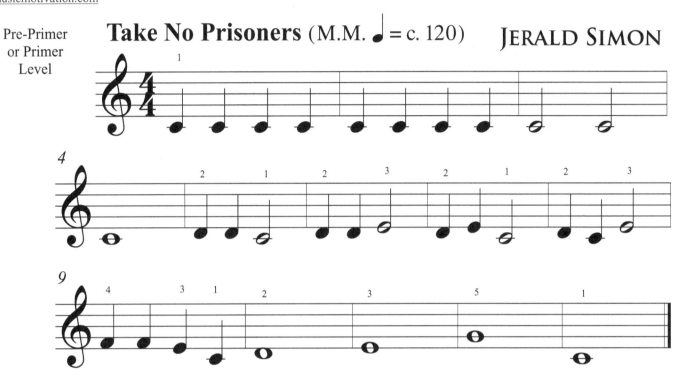

Charlie and Gary are brothers but Gary is very lazy and **C**harlie **D**oes **E**verything **F**or **G**ary!
Gary is so lazy that you only play one G in the entire piece. It's found in measure 12 at the end.
Memorize that phrase to help you remember the names of these five notes: C D E F and G.

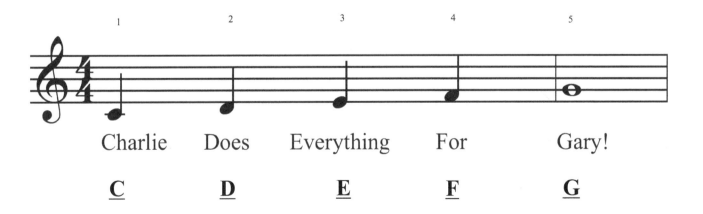

Charlie   Does   Everything   For   Gary!

C   **D**   **E**   **F**   **G**

Dolphins Play Everyday

youtube.com/jeraldsimon
facebook.com/jeraldsimon

Jerald Simon
musicmotivation.com

Skill - We are in the key of C Major. This is a pre-primer/primer level piece for brand new students - especially younger students who are learning the note names. Have FUN playing this "Cool Song"!

Playfully (M.M. ♩ = c. 110)   JERALD SIMON

Pre-Primer
or Primer
Level

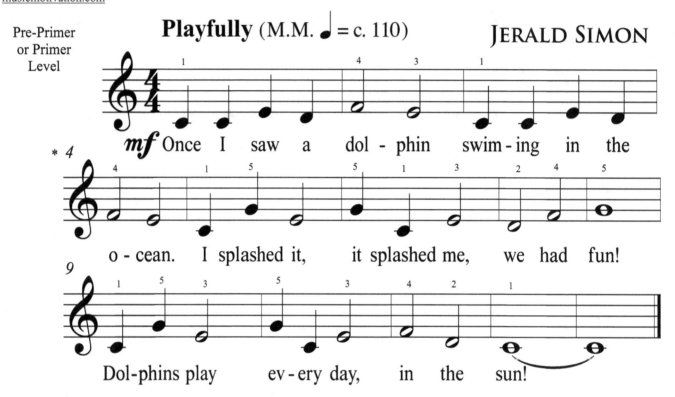

Once I saw a dol - phin swim - ing in the o - cean. I splashed it, it splashed me, we had fun!

Dol-phins play ev - ery day, in the sun!

* For fun try playing an F to a G in measure four instead of the F to an E (it's what I do in the video because I wanted students to choose which note they wanted to play.) I also liked going up since we went down in measure two. You can even switch back and forth from one note to the next.

Charlie and Gary are brothers but Gary is very lazy and **C**harlie **D**oes **E**verything **F**or **G**ary!
Memorize that phrase to help you remember the names of these five notes: C D E F and G.

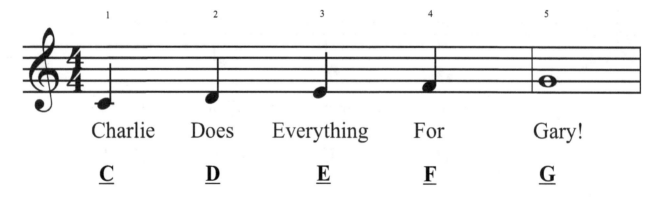

Charlie   Does   Everything   For   Gary!

C   **D**   **E**   **F**   **G**

Feel free to make copies of this and print it off for your piano students. You can make as many copies as you'd like for friends, family, other piano students and also other piano teachers who would like to play this. Have fun playing this "Cool Song"!

THE GAMER

Jerald Simon
musicmotivation.com

This fun "cool song" composed by Jerald Simon, is available to piano teachers and piano students under license with a Cool Songs Beginning Level Package by Jerald Simon. To learn more about Jerald's COOL SONGS and exercises, please visit his website at musicmotivation.com/coolsongs.

This fun "cool song" is in the key of C Major in pentascale position, meaning that the student is only playing the first five notes from the C maor scale. I have several students who love playing video games so I created the orchestration and instrumentation to have video game sound effects and an overall feel of being a "gamer". Have fun playing this!

JERALD SIMON

Like a true "Gamer" would (M.M. ♩ = c. 120)

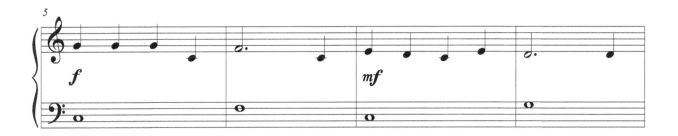

Visit musicmotivation.com/coolsongs to learn more about Jerald's COOL SONGS he composes.

Party

Jerald Simon
musicmotivation.com

Skill - C Major Pentascale: C D E F G (try composing your own composition-LH plays whole notes)

JERALD SIMON

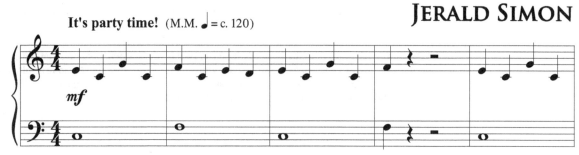

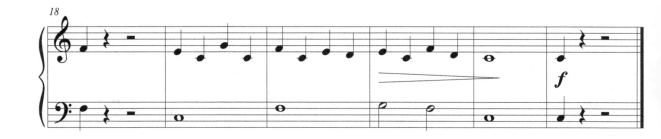

The A Minor ACE

youtube.com/jeraldsimon
facebook.com/jeraldsimon

Skill - We are in the key of A minor. This piece was composed to help students learn the A minor chord and the A minor pentascale (5 note scale). Have FUN playing this "Cool Song"!

Jerald Simon
musicmotivation.com

Late Beginner Level

JERALD SIMON

You've GOT This! ACE it! (M.M. ♩ = c. 100)

Visit musicmotivation.com/coolsongs to learn more about Jerald's COOL SONGS he composes.

sonic

Jerald Simon
musicmotivation.com

This fun "cool song" composed by Jerald Simon, is available to piano teachers and piano students under license with a Cool Songs Early Intermediate Level Package by Jerald Simon. To learn more about Jerald's COOL SONGS and exercises, please visit his website at musicmotivation.com/coolsongs.

This fun "cool song" was created to have students learn a minor chord progression of A minor, F major, and G major. The students practice playing the individual notes, then the octave intervals, followed by the notes as eighth notes, and then as broken fifth intervals, followed by blocked fifth and fourth intervals intervals beginning in measure17. Starting in measure 21, students play the chords in various inversions. Have FUN playing intervals!!

Jerald Simon

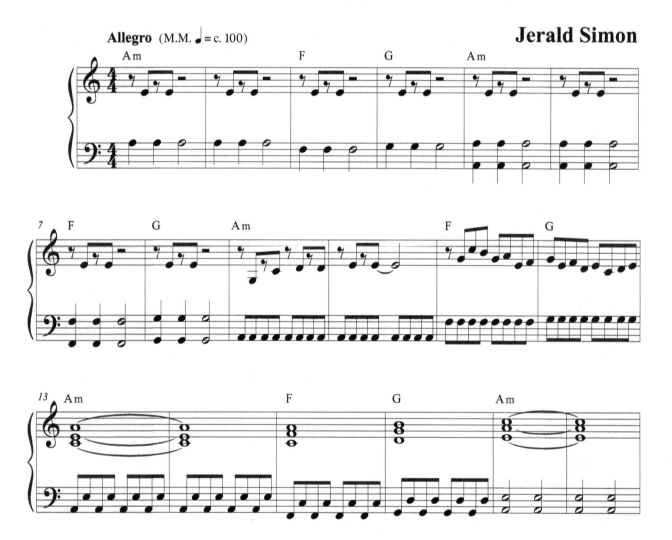

Visit musicmotivation.com/coolsongs to learn more about Jerald's COOL SONGS he composes.

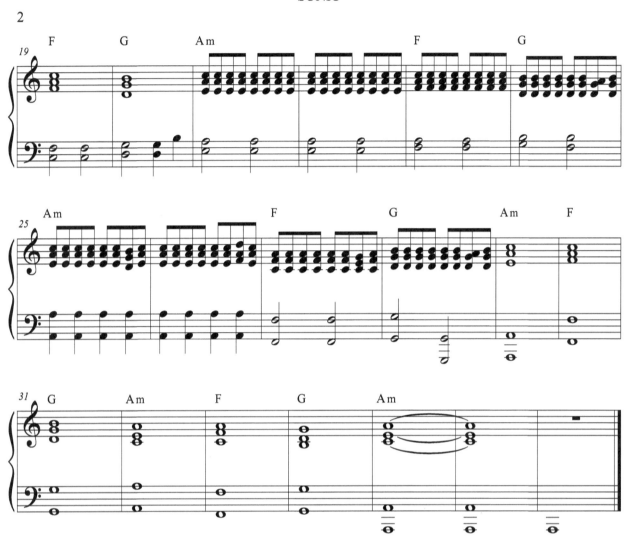

Visit musicmotivation.com/coolsongs to learn more about Jerald's COOL SONGS he composes.

GOOD TIMES

youtube.com/jeraldsimon
facebook.com/jeraldsimon

Skill - Chords created from the C Major Scale - Major, Minor, Minor, Major, Major, Minor, Diminished, Major)
and a Perfect 5th interval with the left hand.

Jerald Simon
musicmotivation.com

JERALD SIMON

Let the Good Times Roll (M.M. ♩= c. 120)

Visit musicmotivation.com/coolsongs to learn more about Jerald's COOL SONGS he composes.

2

Good Times

SPOOK

youtube.com/jeraldsimon
facebook.com/jeraldsimon

Jerald Simon
musicmotivation.com

Skill - Students learn C minor pentascale (C D E flat F and G) and also the first five intervals from the C minor pentascale (prime 1st interval, Major 2nd interval, minor 3rd interval, Perfect 4th, and Perfect 5th intervals as well. To learn more, watch the video of Spook on youtube.com/jeraldsimon

JERALD SIMON

Don't get SPOOKED! (M.M. ♩ = c. 120)

Ped. ad lib
Students write in their own dynamics

2   Spook

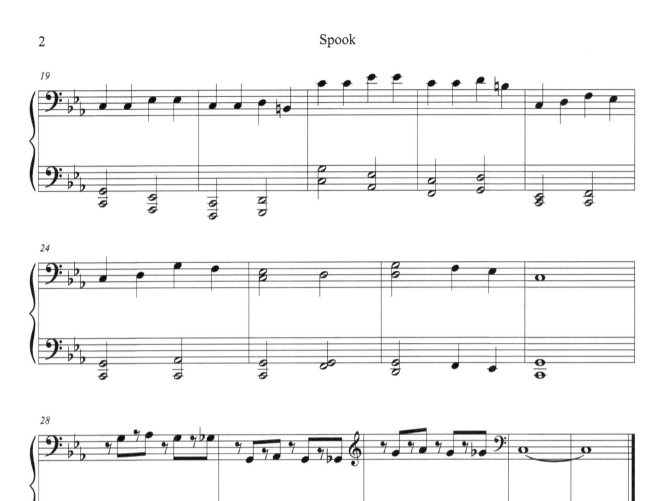

youtube.com/jeraldsimon
facebook.com/jeraldsimon

WHEN SHARKS ATTACK!

JERALD SIMON
musicmotivation.com

This fun "cool song" composed by Jerald Simon, is available to piano teachers and piano students under license with an annual subscription to the weekly "Cool Songs and Cool Exercises by Jerald Simon." To learn more about Jerald's cool weekly songs and exercises, please visit his website at musicmotivation.com/annualsubscription.

This fun "cool song" was created to teach a half step interval (e.g. E to F) to piano students and to help them with a steady quarter note in the left hand (until measure 29) while the right hand plays eighth notes "on beat" and "off beat" with the eighth rests (in measure 9). HAVE FUN!

JERALD SIMON

WATCH OUT!! They're COMING! (M.M. ♩ = c. 120)

Visit musicmotivation.com/coolsongs to learn more about Jerald's COOL SONGS he composes.

2

When Sharks Attack!

youtube.com/jeraldsimon
facebook.com/jeraldsimon

Hybrid-Hero

Jerald Simon
musicmotivation.com

This fun "cool song" composed by Jerald Simon, is available to piano teachers and piano students under license with an annual subscription to the weekly "Cool Songs and Cool Exercises by Jerald Simon." To learn more about Jerald's cool weekly songs and exercises, please visit his website at musicmotivation.com/annualsubscription.

This fun "cool song" was created to help students learn to keep rhythmn with competing eighth notes and eighth rests between the right and left hand. Have FUN playing this chord progression!

Jerald Simon

Allegro (M.M. ♩= c. 120)

Visit musicmotivation.com/coolsongs to learn more about Jerald's COOL SONGS he composes.

Hybrid-Hero

Can you name the intervals from measures 24-32 with the right hand?

The Labyrinth

Skill - We are in the key of D minor using the 6/8 time signature. The left hand primarily plays octave intervals while the right hand creates the interesting melody line. The right hand plays a combination of eighth and sixthteenth notes moving up and down using the notes from the D minor scale. Have fun with this one!

Jerald Simon
musicmotivation.com

JERALD SIMON

Are You Lost? Do You Know Where You Are? (M.M. ♩ = c. 65)

Students write in their own dynamics!

2

The Labyrinth

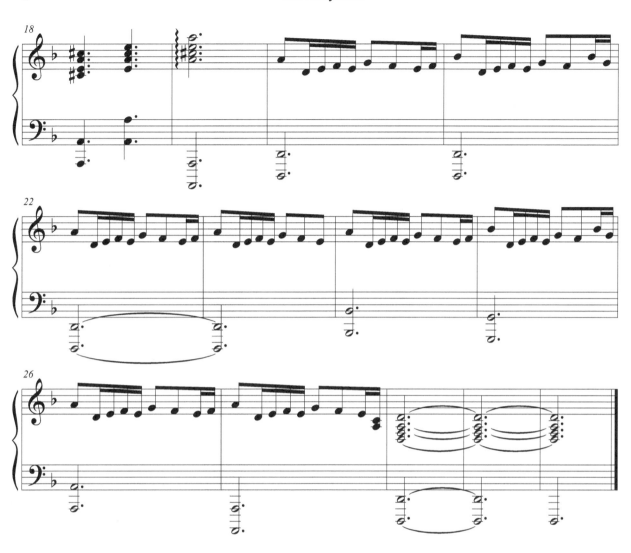

Visit musicmotivation.com/coolsongs to learn more about Jerald's COOL SONGS he composes.

Boulevard

youtube.com/jeraldsimon
facebook.com/jeraldsimon

Skill - We are in the key of C major. We are working on a simple left hand pattern and
Have FUN playing this "Cool Song"!

Jerald Simon
musicmotivation.com

Techno-Pop Feel (♩ = c. 120)

JERALD SIMON

Student's can write in their own dynamics!

Intermediate
Level

Visit musicmotivation.com/coolsongs to learn more about Jerald's COOL SONGS he composes.

Boulevard

Boulevard

A Few Additional Ideas for Piano Teachers and Parents of Piano Students

You can visit this link to read the original blog post from which this presentation was created: (https://www.musicmotivation.com/blog/don-t-teach-music-theory-unless-you-teach-the-practical-application).

In the blog post, I talked specifically about 10 steps to begin teaching the practical application of music theory so students know their theory inside and out. I thought I would share the 10 steps here from the blog post:

Before any piano student plays their piece, I believe they should be able to do the following (this is what I try to have my students do with their music):

1. Tell their music teacher the key signature and time signature.

2. Identify all of the sharps or flats in the key signature.

3. Play all of the intervals created from the major key signature of the piece they are playing - this is more for piano students and possibly guitar students, as many instruments only allow one note at a time. If the student is younger or new to their instrument, they can play the intervals created from the pentascales or five note scales created from the first five notes of the major or minor scales.

4. Play through the major scale of the key signature of the piece at least 1-2 octaves up and down the piano (parallel and or contrary motion). If the student is younger or new to their instrument, as stated before, they can play the pentascales, or five note scales created from the first five notes of the major or minor scales.

5. Play what I refer to as the "Essential Piano Exercises" from each key signature. (In the blog post I show an example from the key of C major from my book "Essential Piano Exercises" - Intervals, Scales, and Chords in all Keys and in all Inversions - a 288 page book with all intervals, scales, and simple triads and 6th and 7th chords in all keys and inversions).

These are the other 5 steps:

Once a student can do the above five essential "getting started steps" in any given key signature (and many times I will do the following steps even if they can't do the above steps in every key signature), I then challenge them to do the following five essential "music theory application steps."

1. Once the student has learned and perfected the piece, ask him or her to take the song up half a step and down half a step. In the beginning, this is a good start. Later on, when they are better able to do so, have the student play the piece in any key signature. Start with simple pieces like "Mary Had a Little Lamb" and "Twinkle, Twinkle, Little Star." Have the students try playing these in all key signatures.

2. Ask the student to come up with at least 5-10 variations or arrangements of their piece.

3. Ask the student to compose 3 or 4 motifs (or single melodic line or phrase), and then put them together. This can be the beginning of creating a simple piece. I have students begin using scales and skipping notes here and there. We then have them take a simple pattern created from the notes of the major scale (1 2 3 4 5 6 7 8).

4. Ask the student to "Play a Rainbow." When I say this to students, I then begin to ask them to "play" anything. I may say: "Play me a shadow," "Play me a swing set," or "Play me a thunderstorm," "Play me a puddle, a rock, a tree, a meadow, a light, etc.". The sky is the limit. I first begin with tangible objects and eventually move on to intangible ideas and concepts: "Play me loneliness," "Play me disturbed, agitated, angered, humbled, pensive, etc.". Again, the sky is the limit. It is wonderful to see what students can create, even if they don't know all the rules of composition or terminology. Everyone has music within them.

5. I have students begin notating their music. I enjoy and prefer Finale, but that is because I have used it for so long and am familiar with it. There are many great programs available. After we have their music put down on paper, I then export the music from Finale as a midi file and open the midi file in Logic Pro. We then begin having them add additional instruments so they can create background tracks (this is how I create all of my weekly "**Cool Songs**" from my **COOL SONGS Series** (you can learn more about my COOL SONGS Series at this link: https://musicmotivation.com/coolsongs/). The students then have a PDF copy of their composition and an MP3 "minus track" to accompany them as they play. Talk about music motivation!

These are the books included in the COOL SONGS Series: https://musicmotivation.com/coolsongs/ -

The Apprentice Stage - The Maestro Stage - The Virtuoso Stage

COOL SONGS for COOL KIDS (Primer Level) by Jerald Simon
COOL SONGS for COOL KIDS (book 1) by Jerald Simon
COOL SONGS for COOL KIDS (book 2) by Jerald Simon
COOL SONGS for COOL KIDS (book 3) by Jerald Simon
COOL SONGS that ROCK! (book 1) by Jerald Simon
COOL SONGS that ROCK! (book 2) by Jerald Simon

Join the **Essential Piano Exercises Course** by Jerald Simon
https://www.essentialpianoexercises.com

Gain lifetime access to the PDF books listed below (which also includes video piano lesson tutorials where Jerald Simon demonstrates examples from the books and gives piano pointers, tips to try, and the practical application of music theory). Jerald demonstrates how to use the music theory to arrange and compose music of your own!

This course features pre-recorded video lessons so you can watch and learn how to play the piano at your convenience. You choose when and where you learn to play the piano.

Join the **Essential Piano Exercises Course** and receive the following PDF books along with access to the monthly video lesson taught by Jerald Simon for a one time payment of $199.95.

Join the **Essential Piano Exercises Course** by Jerald Simon

EssentialPianoExercises.com

Gain lifetime access to the following PDF books (which include video piano lesson tutorials where Jerald Simon demonstrates examples from the book and gives piano pointers, tips to try, and the practical application of music theory where Jerald demonstrates how to use the music theory!

This course features pre-recorded video lessons so you can watch and learn how to play the piano at your convenience. You choose when and where you learn to play the piano.

This Course features the following books (included as PDF downloads with the course):

1. **Essential Piano Exercises Every Piano Player Should Know - PDF book and Video Course**
2. **100 Left Hand Patterns Every Piano Player Should Know - PDF book and Video Course**
3. **Essential Jazz Piano Exercises Every Piano Player Should Know - PDF book and Video Course**
4. **Essential New Age Piano Exercises Every Piano Player Should Know - PDF book and Video Course**
5. **100 Chord Progressions Every Piano Player Should Know - PDF book and Video Course**
6. **Jazzed about Jazz - PDF book and Video Course**
7. **Jazzed about Christmas - PDF book and Video Course**
8. **Jazzed about 4th of July - PDF book and Video Course**
9. **Fake Book FUNdamentals - Getting Started with using Fakebooks at the piano**
10. **Innovative Improvisation Ideas Every Piano Player Should Know - PDF book and Video Course**

In addition to having access to these PDF books and Video Courses, the following will be added to your lifetime account:

- After January 1st, 2021 new material will continue to be added on Mondays and Fridays as before, but will only be available for monthly members who have a subscription to access the new materials added each month ($29.95 per month for a monthly subscription). Anyone who has purchased the Essential Piano Exercises course will continue to have access to all of the PDF books, video lesson tutorials, power point presentations, and handouts. New books, additional MP3s, new video lessons, and monthly training seminars, webinars, and additional resources will be added for the current members of the Essential Piano Exercises monthly subscription group.
- Access to the Essential Piano Exercises Facebook group - a private Facebook group created only for the members of the Essential Piano Exercises course. By joining the Facebook group you will have access to additional live piano lessons every week taught by Jerald Simon. Weekly piano pointers, tips to try, and short video lessons will be shared throughout the week for the members of the Facebook group.

Join the COOL SONGS Club and start using my COOL SONGS Series...

If you would like to learn more about the COOL SONGS Series I created to help motivate and inspire piano students - especially during their teenage years, you can visit my website: **https://musicmotivation.com/coolsongs**.

I compose COOL SONGS to help motivate and inspire piano students!

Parents praise COOL SONGS, piano teachers rave about them, and piano students can't wait to play them! Every piano recital instantly turns into a COOL concert when students perform COOL SONGS.

There are three ways to start using the COOL SONGS I have composed continually compose each week.

1. If you haven't already, visit this link to download my FREE COOL SONGS Starter package (12 FREE COOL SONGS with accompaniment minus tracks: **http://coolsongsclub. com/freebook**. There are 4 beginning level, 4 early intermediate level, and 4 intermediate - advanced level COOL SONGS) so you can start using my COOL SONGS (these are actually the same ones I have included in this book, but you will be able to download the accompaniment MP3 minus tracks and watch the video lessons as well). You will also receive my FREE 130 page PDF Book: "20 Ways to Motivate Teen Piano Students to Want to Play the Piano - the FUN WAY!" and be signed up to receive my FREE Weekly PDF Piano Lesson Outline (emailed out every Monday).

2. If you'd like to purchase the COOL SONGS Series, you can visit this link to Purchase the entire COOL SONGS Series Course single use license (Over 4 years worth of piano lessons - 163 COOL SONGS complete with video lessons and accompaniment MP3 minus tracks) for a one time payment of $49.95: https://www.coolsongsclub.com/order. You'll have lifetime access to all of the COOL SONGS in the series (piano teachers will also be able to upgrade their single use license to a lifetime piano teacher studio license if they'd like to when checking out).

3. Once you have purchased the COOL SONGS Series for $49.95 and/or upgraded to a studio license if you are a piano teacher, you will then be able to join the COOL SONGS Club as either a piano teacher or piano student. This is a monthly subscription club for $6.95 per month. All COOL SONGS Club members receive new COOL SONGS and COOL EXERCISES every month (everything is a studio license so teachers can reprint the music out for students). If you are a piano student, you do not need to purchase the studio license.

Download this **FREE PDF book** -
"20 Ways to Motivate Teen Piano Students to Want to Play the Piano" at:
https://www.musicmotivation.com/optin.

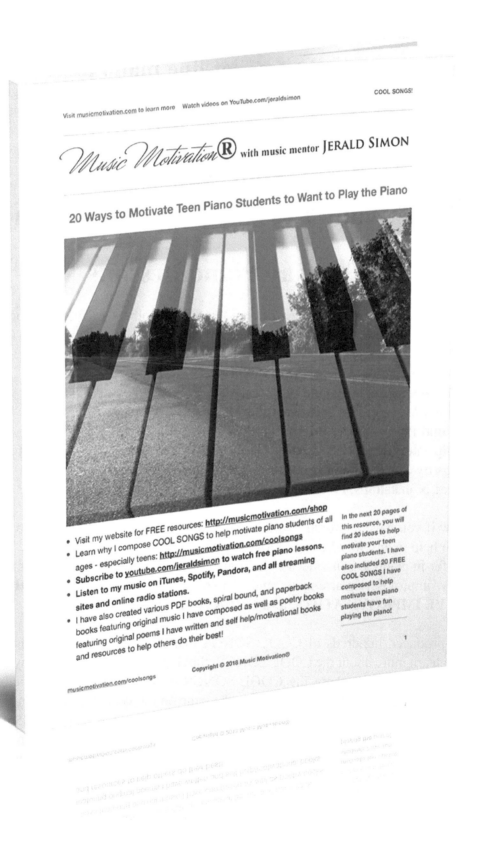

Subscribe to my YouTube Channel:

youtube.com/jeraldsimon

I upload new videos on Wednesdays, and Fridays on my YouTube channel, **youtube.com/jeraldsimon**. I have a few different playlists filled with great content for beginning - advanced piano students. The videos are geared for everyone from brand new piano students to music majors, professional pianists, and piano teachers of all skill levels.

There are three main playlists for my **free on-line piano lessons.** I do offer in person piano lessons, Zoom/FaceTime piano lessons, and step by step piano lesson packages you can purchase and watch at home (https://www.musicmotivation.com/pianolessons), but the ones listed below are FREE to everyone who subscribes to my YouTube channel:

1. **PIANO FUNdamentals** (emphasis on the word FUN!)
2. **5 Minute Piano Lessons with Jerald Simon** (sponsored by Music Motivation®)
3. **Theory Tip Tuesday Piano Lessons**

I frequently release new videos. Some are piano lessons, and others are filmed recordings of workshops, masterclasses, or concerts. I also have these additional types of videos on my YouTube channel:

a. Meditation/Relaxation Music Composed by Jerald Simon
b. Hymn Arrangements by Jerald Simon
c. Motivational Messages by Jerald Simon
d. Motivational Poetry by Jerald Simon
e. Theory Tip Tuesday (FREE Weekly Piano Lesson Videos) by Jerald Simon
f. Cool Songs by Jerald Simon (musicmotivation.com/coolsongs)
g. Assemblies, Workshops, Firesides, and more...

Let me know if you have a tutorial you'd like me to come out with to better help you learn the piano. I'm happy to help in any way I can and love hearing feedback from others about what they personally are looking for in piano lesson videos to help them learn to play the piano better. I primarily focus on music theory, improvisation/arranging, and composition. I refer to these as **THEORY THERAPY, INNOVATIVE IMPROVISATION, and CREATIVE COMPOSITION**.

I have also produced hundreds of COOL SONGS that teach students music theory the fun way. If you'd like to learn more about the COOL SONGS, that I composed to motivate my own piano students, or if you would like to purchase the COOL SONGS series featuring the music/books, simply visit musicmotivation.com/coolsongs to be taken to the page on my website that explains a little more about the COOL SONGS. You can also watch piano video tutorial lessons featuring 85 of the 200 + COOL SONGS (youtube.com/jeraldsimon). Let me know what you think. I'd love your feedback about the music. It helps me as I compose more COOL SONGS to motivate more piano students. I'm excited to have you watch my free video piano lessons on YouTube.com/jeraldsimon.

Perceptions, Parables, and Pointers by JERALD SIMON (read more at this link): http://musicmotivation. com/shop/motivationalself-help-books/perceptions-parables-and-pointers-by-jerald-simon/

What do you really want to do with your time? What is your mission in life? Where have you been, and where would you like to go? What are your dreams, your hopes, and your wishes? If you could do anything in the world, what would it be?

The main goal in writing down these perceptions, parables, and pointers, and in creating this book in general, is to present ideas that will help get people thinking, imagining, planning, creating, and actively participating in life.

The "As If" Principle (motivational poetry) by JERALD SIMON features 222 original motivational poems written by Simon to inspire and motivate men, women, businesses, organizations, leaders, mentors, advisers, teachers, and students. The poems were written to teach values and encourage everyone everywhere to do and be their best. (read more at this link): http://musicmotivation.com/shop/motivationalself-help-books/the-as-if-principle-by-jerald-simon/

CHECK OUT JERALD'S MOTIVATIONAL BOOKS

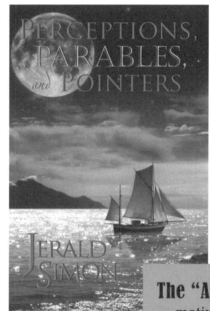

PERCEPTIONS, PARABLES, AND POINTERS
$19.95

216 PAGES

A SELF–HELP MOTIVATION MANUAL

MOTIVATION IN A MINUTE
$18.95

FULL COLOR PICTURES AND MOTIVATIONAL MESSAGES

THE "AS IF" PRINCIPLE
(MOTIVATIONAL POETRY)
$16.95

154 PAGES

222 INSPIRATIONAL AND MOTIVATIONAL POEMS WRITTEN BY JERALD

ALL BOOKS ARE AVAILABLE ON AMAZON, BARNES AND NOBLE, AND ALL ONLINE AND TRADITIONAL BOOK STORES

Jerald's Albums & Singles
are available from all online music stores

Stream Jerald's music on
Pandora, Spotify, iTunes, Amazon, and all streaming sites.

Music Books, Albums, MP3s, Self Help and Motivational Books, Poetry Books and YouTube Videos
Check out my books and music on **iTunes, Amazon, Spotify, Pandora,** & **YouTube.com/jeraldsimon**
Motivate Piano Students! Music Motivation® - P.O. Box 1000 - Kaysville, UT 84037-1000

Check out Jerald's Cool Song Piano Packages

Jerald continually produces and releases new "Cool Songs" available for all piano students and piano teachers on his website (*musicmotivation.com*). Each new "*Cool Song*" is emailed to Music Motivation® mentees (piano teachers and piano students) who have enrolled in the "COOL SONGS" monthly subscription program. See which subscription is the best fit for you and for your piano students (if you are a piano teacher) by visiting:

http://musicmotivation.com/coolsongs

At **Music Motivation®**, I strive to produce the best quality products I can to help musicians of all ages better understand music theory (Theory Therapy), improvisation (Innovative Improvisation), and composition (Creative Composition). I try to tailor my products around the needs of piano teachers and piano students of all ages - from beginning through advanced and would love to receive your feedback about what I can do to better help you teach and learn. Let me know if there is a type of piano music, music book, fun audio or video tutorial, or any other educational product you would like to see in the field of music (principally the piano), but have not yet found, that would help you teach and learn the piano better. Please contact me. I look forward to your comments and suggestions. Thank you.

Check out these best sellers by Jerald Simon

visit *musicmotivation.com* to purchase, or visit your local music store - Chesbro music is the national distributor for all Music Motivation® books. Contact Chesbro Music Co. if you are a store (1.800.243.7276)

Learn more about
JERALD SIMON

Visit https://www.musicmotivation.com/jeraldsimon

"My purpose and mission in life is to motivate myself and others through my music and writing, to help others find their purpose and mission in life, and to teach values and encourage everyone everywhere to do and be their best." - Jerald Simon

First and foremost, Jerald is a husband to his beautiful wife, Zanny, and a father to his wonderful children. Jerald Simon is the founder of **Music Motivation®** (musicmotivation.com), a company he formed to provide music instruction through workshops, giving speeches and seminars, concerts and performances in the field of music and motivation. He is a composer, author, poet, and Music Mentor/piano teacher (primarily focusing his piano teaching on music theory, improvisation, composition, and arranging). Jerald loves spending time with his wife, Zanny, and their children. In addition, he loves music, teaching, speaking, performing, playing sports, exercising, reading, writing poetry and self help books, and gardening.

Jerald Simon is the founder of **Music Motivation®** and focuses on helping piano students and piano teachers learn music theory, improvisation, and composition. He refers to these areas as: **Theory Therapy™, Innovative Improvisation™, and Creative Composition™.** Simon is an author and composer and has written 30 music books featuring almost 300 original compositions, 15 albums (you can listen to Jerald's music on Pandora, Spotify, iTunes, Amazon, and all online music stations. Jerald's books and CDs are also available from Amazon, Wal-Mart.com, Barnes and Noble and all major retail outlets). He has published three motivational poetry books featuring over 400 original poems (poetrythatmotivates.com), and is the creator of the best-selling **Cool Songs Series** (musicmotivation.com/coolsongs), the best-selling **Essential Piano Exercises Series** (essentialpianoexercises.com) and Essential Piano Lessons for piano students (essentialpianolessons.com). He has also created **Essential Piano Teachers** for piano teachers (essentialpianoteachers.com). You can watch Jerald's videos on his YouTube channel at: youtube.com/jeraldsimon. Listen to Jerald's music on all streaming sites and his podcast, **Music, Motivation, and More – The Positivity Podcast** with Jerald Simon on all podcast platforms.

In 2008, Jerald began creating his Cool Songs to help teach music theory – the FUN way, by putting FUN back into theory FUNdamentals. Jerald has also filmed hundreds of piano lesson video tutorials on his YouTube page (youtube.com/jeraldsimon). In addition to music books and albums, he is the author/poet of **"The As If Principle"** (motivational poetry), and the books **"Perceptions, Parables, and Pointers," "Motivation in a Minute,"** and **"Who Are You?"**.

SPECIALTIES:

Composer, Author, Poet, Music Mentor, Piano Teacher (jazz, music theory, improvisation, composition, arranging, etc.), Motivational Speaker, and Life Coach. Visit **https://www.musicmotivation.com/**, to book Jerald as a speaker/performer. Visit **https://www.musicmotivation.com/** to print off FREE piano resources for piano teachers and piano students.

Book me to speak/perform for your group or for a concert or performance:

jeraldsimon@musicmotivation.com - **(801)644-0540** - https://www.musicmotivation.com/

Made in United States
Troutdale, OR
12/05/2024

25972568R00164